Sovereign Debt Structure for Crisis Prevention

**Eduardo Borensztein, Marcos Chamon, Olivier Jeanne,
Paolo Mauro, and Jeromin Zettelmeyer**

INTERNATIONAL MONETARY FUND
Washington DC
2004

© 2004 International Monetary Fund

Production: IMF Multimedia Services Division
Figures: Jorge Salazar
Typesetting: Alicia Etchebarne-Bourdin

Cataloging-in-Publication Data

Sovereign debt structure for crisis prevention/Eduardo Borensztein . . . [et al.]—
Washington, D.C.: International Monetary Fund, 2004.

    p. cm.—(Occasional paper); 237

    Includes bibliographical references.
    ISBN 1-58906-377-5

    1. Debts, public. 2. Financial instruments. I. Borensztein, Eduardo. II. Occasional paper (International Monetary Fund); no. 237.

HJ8011.S68 2004

Price: US$25.00
(US$22.00 to full-time faculty members and
students at universities and colleges)

Please send orders to:
International Monetary Fund, Publication Services
700 19th Street, N.W., Washington, D.C. 20431, U.S.A.
Tel.: (202) 623-7430   Telefax: (202) 623-7201
E-mail: publications@imf.org
Internet: http://www.imf.org

recycled paper

Contents

Preface   vii

I   Overview   I

    Two Views on the Status Quo   1
    Debt Structures with Existing Instruments: Emerging Market
        Countries Versus Advanced Economies   3
    Ideas for Sovereigns from the Corporate Context: Explicit Seniority   3
    Expanding the Set of Instruments: Real Indexation   4
    Toward Better Sovereign Debt Structures: A Road Map   5

II   Facts on Existing Public Debt Structures   7

    Public Debt in Emerging Market Countries Versus Advanced
        Economies   7
    Sovereign Versus Corporate Liability Structures   11

**III   Rendering Debt Structures Less Crisis Prone with Existing
       Instruments**   14

    Problems with the Status Quo   14
    Determinants of Government Debt Structure   15
    Policy Implications   19

IV   Explicit Seniority in Privately Held Sovereign Debt   23

    Economic Role of Seniority   23
    Approaches and Obstacles in Implementing Explicit Seniority   25
    Conclusions   28

**V   Expanding the Set of Instruments: Indexation to
       Real Variables**   29

    Benefits of Indexation to Real Variables   29
    Real Variables Beyond the Control of the Country's Authorities   31
    Real Variables Partially Within the Control of the Country's
        Authorities   38
    Obstacles for Variables Partly Within the Control of the Government   42
    Steps to Foster Acceptance   43
    Real Indexation: Which Variables for Which Countries?   44

VI   Past and Future of Innovation in Sovereign Borrowing   46

    Financial Innovation in Sovereign Borrowing: A Haphazard Process   46
    Road Maps for Future Innovation   48

VII   Conclusions   49

Appendix Investors' Attitudes Toward Growth-Linked and Other Innovative Financial Instruments for Sovereign Borrowers: Results of a Survey — 51

References — 56

Boxes

1. Debt Structure and Hedging — 17
2. Creating Domestic Markets for Long-Term Domestic-Currency Bonds: Country Experiences — 20
3. Developing International Markets for Bonds in Emerging Market Currencies — 21
4. Enforcing Contractual Seniority — 26
5. Effect on Borrowing Costs of a Switch to First-in-Time Seniority — 27
6. Proposals for Indexation to Real Variables — 30
7. Benefits of GDP Indexation for Emerging Markets and Advanced Economies — 41
8. Previous Examples of Indexation to Real Variables — 43

Text Tables

1. External Sovereign Debt: Currency Composition, 1980–2003 — 10
2. Structure of Domestically Issued Government Bonds at End-2001 — 10
3. Structure of Total (Domestic and External) Central Government Debt, 2001 — 12
4. Percentage Share of the Top Three Exports in Total Exports, 1990–99 — 32
5. Top Five Natural Disasters by Percent of GDP Lost — 34
6. Small Countries: Types of Disasters, 1975–2002 — 36
7. Output Growth and Trading Partners' Growth, 1970–2002 — 38
8. Introduction of Inflation-Indexed Securities by Sovereigns — 47

Text Figures

1. Advanced Economies and Emerging Market Countries: Public Debt Stocks and Debt Composition — 7
2. Structure of External Public Debt in Emerging Market Countries — 8
3. Emerging Market Countries: Fixed- Versus Floating-Rate Sovereign Bond Issues — 8
4. Structure of Internationally Issued Debt: Maturity Composition — 9
5. Emerging Market Countries: Structure of Public Debt — 11
6. All Developing Countries: Public Sector Bonds and Loans Issued in International Markets — 13
7. Recent Crises: Impact of Exchange Rate Depreciation on Public Debt-to-GDP Ratio — 15
8. Share of Long-Term Local-Currency Bonds in Total Government Domestic Bonds and Inflation History — 16
9. Share of Long-Term Local-Currency Bonds and Financial Liberalization — 18
10. Institutional Quality and Domestically Issued Long-Term Local-Currency Debt — 19
11. Interest Savings over the Economic Cycle — 40

Appendix Tables

A1. Question 3: Obstacles to Growth-Linked Bonds   53
A2. Question 4: Obstacles to Growth-Linked Bonds   54
A3. Question 5: Obstacles to Commodity-Indexed Bonds   54
A4. Question 6: Obstacles to Domestic-Currency Bonds   54

Appendix Figures

A1. Question 1: Premium over Plain Vanilla Bonds   52
A2. Question 2: Premium over Plain Vanilla Bonds   53

The following symbols have been used throughout this paper:

. . .   to indicate that data are not available;

—   to indicate that the figure is zero or less than half the final digit shown, or that the item does not exist;

–   between years or months (e.g., 2001–02 or January–June) to indicate the years or months covered, including the beginning and ending years or months;

/   between years (e.g., 2001/02) to indicate a fiscal (financial) year.

"n.a." means not applicable.

"Billion" means a thousand million.

Minor discrepancies between constituent figures and totals are due to rounding.

The term "country," as used in this paper, does not in all cases refer to a territorial entity that is a state as understood by international law and practice; the term also covers some territorial entities that are not states, but for which statistical data are maintained and provided internationally on a separate and independent basis.

Preface

This Occasional Paper is intended to stimulate debate on the issue of sovereign debt structures for crisis prevention. It was prepared under the general guidance of Raghuram Rajan. The authors include Eduardo Borensztein, Marcos Chamon, Olivier Jeanne, Paolo Mauro, and Jeromin Zettelmeyer. Work on the paper was led by Paolo Mauro. The authors are grateful to Jonathan Ostry, Anna Gelpern, Sean Hagan, Simon Johnson, Thomas Laryea, and several other colleagues for helpful comments; to Priyanka Malhotra and Martin Minnoni for excellent research assistance; and to Usha David for editorial assistance. Special thanks to Leslie Payton-Jacobs of EMTA for helpful suggestions and cooperation in circulating the survey, and to Kellett Hannah for web services. Archana Kumar of the External Relations Department edited the paper and coordinated its production.

The opinions expressed are solely those of the authors and do not necessarily reflect the views of the International Monetary Fund or its Executive Directors.

I Overview

The way countries structure their public borrowing has long been considered an important determinant of economic performance. This topic has recently received renewed attention as a result of not only steep increases in public debt levels in emerging market countries—and a number of highly visible and damaging crises—but also pronounced changes in the composition of those debts.[1] There is increasing recognition that debt structure has important implications for both the frequency of crises and the disruption they cause when they strike.[2] Indeed, the official sector is beginning to give renewed prominence to the possible need for innovations in the design of countries' financial liabilities.[3]

The debate on government debt in the context of possible reforms of the international financial architecture has thus far focused on crisis resolution.[4] This Occasional Paper seeks to broaden the debate by asking how government debt could be structured to pursue other objectives, including crisis prevention, international risk-sharing, and facilitating the adjustment of fiscal variables to changes in domestic economic conditions. To that end, this paper considers recently developed analytical approaches to improving the structure of sovereign debt using existing debt instruments. It then reviews a number of proposals—including the introduction of explicit seniority and GDP-linked instruments—in the sovereign context and discusses their pros and cons, and the related practical challenges.

While recognizing that there is no easy substitute for sound macroeconomic policies—fiscal policies in particular—and that no amount of financial engineering could eliminate crises, this paper asks whether greater use of relatively underutilized financial instruments could help reduce the frequency of damaging crises. After identifying common sources of vulnerability, the paper takes a first pass at identifying instruments and structures that could help achieve a more resilient debt structure, and sets forth some preliminary considerations about their feasibility.

Two Views on the Status Quo

Developing a strategy for addressing possible inefficiencies in existing debt structures requires an understanding of what may cause them. On this subject, there are two views in the policy and academic debate. The first, which underlies most proposals for reforming the "international financial architecture," assumes that today's array of instruments is inherited from historical accident and has persisted owing to inertia: the existing structures can be changed, though not without substantial effort, through reforms involving coordination among market participants. The second view argues that the status quo is an adaptation to deeper problems, such as difficulties in enforcing contracts in the international setting, lack of policy credibility, and weaknesses in domestic institutions. The outcome may well be inefficient, but it cannot be improved without addressing the underlying problems.

History and Inertia

The "architecture" analogy is one of a house whose current form results from the way it was built in the past, in response to incentives or needs that may have had little to do with those of its present inhabitants. Under this view, making a case for reform merely requires showing that the architecture gives rise to costly and inefficient outcomes. Of course, structures that are considered part of the

---

Note: The authors of this section are Paolo Mauro and Jeromin Zettelmeyer.

[1]International Monetary Fund and World Bank (2001 and 2003); IMF, *World Economic Outlook* (September 2003, Chapter 3); Reinhart, Rogoff, and Savastano (2003); Guidotti and Kumar (1991).

[2]International Monetary Fund (2003a); and Allen and others (2002).

[3]The Declaration of Nuevo León (Special Summit of the Americas, Monterrey, Mexico, January 2004) supports "the efforts of borrowing countries to work with the private sector to explore new approaches to reduce the burden of debt service during periods of economic downturns" (available via the Internet: www.summit-americas.org/SpecialSummit/declaration_monterrey-eng.htm).

[4]International Monetary Fund (2003b).

architecture do not generally change by themselves: this requires a reform effort. But the good news is that through such an effort, most structures can be torn down and rebuilt, or at least renovated and cleaned.

Changes to the status quo could however be difficult to achieve for many reasons, especially a need for coordination among market participants. For individual market participants, it is hard to go against market practice in drafting contracts. Moreover, reforms often require mustering support from national parliaments, international bodies, or market participants. A number of potential obstacles thus stand in the way of contractual or financial innovation (Allen and Gale, 1994):

- *Coordination problems and the need to ensure "critical mass" for new instruments.* The appeal of an innovation often depends on its simultaneous adoption by many contracting parties. For example, learning to price new financial instruments may require excessive resources from the viewpoint of an individual investor, but may be worth the effort collectively for the potential investor class. More generally, individual borrowers considering whether to issue a new financial instrument will not take into account the benefits for other borrowers and investors that would result from establishing a new asset class. And in the absence of a concerted effort to guarantee a minimum critical mass, investors may be concerned about the possibility of limited liquidity for the new instruments and thus demand a "novelty premium."

- *The highly competitive structure of financial markets.* A private financial institution would have to incur costs to develop a new type of financial instrument. However, it may be unable to maintain a monopoly over the provision of this instrument for a long time: patents are still rarely (though increasingly) used for financial instruments, and imitation is relatively easy. Thus, the private incentive to develop the instrument in the first place may be low, even if its social benefit may be high.

- *The need for standards.* To create a liquid secondary market where investors can easily diversify their portfolio, it is important to have instruments with the same features for all countries or all firms issuing them. Moreover, for financial instruments where payments are due when certain conditions are met, it is crucial to have verifiable standards for whether those conditions are met. For example, the market for credit default swaps remained small for years but took off as soon as the standards for a

"credit event" were properly defined and became broadly accepted.[5]

- *Signaling.* Individual countries may be reluctant to issue new financial instruments or existing instruments with new contractual features if they fear that such innovations may be misperceived as signs of weakness or lack of commitment to good policies.

Deeper Problems

An alternative view is that prevailing contracts and market practices result from the responses of creditors and sovereign debtors to deeper problems, including difficulties in enforcing contracts involving sovereign borrowers, and the possibility of moral hazard (behavior that does not maximize the likelihood of repayment) on the part of debtors. Costly debt crises may look inefficient ex post but are, in this view, the only way to discourage defaults (Dooley, 2000; Dooley and Verma, 2001). Existing debt instruments are seen as optimal because they imply that crises will occasionally occur to constrain or discipline borrowing governments. Similarly, "risky" and seemingly inefficient debt structures heavily weighted toward foreign-currency-denominated debt and short-term debt are rationalized as necessary evils to reduce moral hazard on the part of policymakers, or minimize debt dilution (Chamon, 2002; Jeanne, 2000, 2004; Tirole, 2002; and Sections II and III).[6] Thus, crisis-prone debt structures can be a symptom rather than the root cause of countries' inability to commit to good policies; such inability may in turn result from weak domestic institutions.

Under this view, attempts to reform the international financial architecture by changing outcomes but without addressing underlying distortions could well be counterproductive. For example, restrictions or taxes on short-term debt might seek to induce a move from short-term to long-term flows. However, their impact might be undone by international investors' shift toward other forms of debt that are similarly difficult to dilute, such as foreign-currency debt. Alternatively, if the impact of the restrictions cannot be undone, they might end up reducing or eliminating capital flows altogether. As in Oscar Wilde's *Canterville Ghost*, for the stain to cease from reappearing on the carpet the next morning, it is not enough to apply the latest carpet cleaner. The ghost itself must be laid to rest.

---

[5]Credit default swaps are instruments giving the holder the right to sell a bond at its face value in the event of default by the issuer.

[6]The disciplining role of short-term and other risky forms of debt has also been emphasized in the corporate context (Calomiris and Kahn, 1991; Diamond, 1991).

Both interpretations of the status quo have some merit, and this paper draws upon them in the subsequent sections. The focus on underlying causes of inefficiencies in existing debt structures leads to a discussion of associated policy and institutional failures, and remedies for them. Beyond this, though, and recognizing that crises are exceedingly costly,[7] this paper provides a preliminary analysis of the case for innovations that could directly improve sovereign debt structures, but may have been impeded in the past primarily by inertia.

Debt Structures with Existing Instruments: Emerging Market Countries Versus Advanced Economies

In analyzing existing debt structures, two sets of comparisons provide insights into how debt structures might be improved (Section II). First, a comparison between debt structures in emerging market countries and advanced economies highlights characteristics that make advanced economies less crisis prone. Second, a comparison between sovereigns and corporates highlights the roles of equity and seniority in corporate liability structures, with potential applications in the sovereign context.

Compared with advanced economies, emerging market and developing countries find it relatively difficult to issue long-term debt in their own currencies. Greater reliance on short-term and foreign-currency debt is associated with a higher frequency of debt crises (Section III). Short-term debt (or debt indexed to short-term domestic interest rates) is associated with vulnerability to sudden changes in market sentiment: worsening perceptions of the country's creditworthiness can quickly feed into higher interest costs, often leading to vicious circles. Similarly, with relatively large shares of foreign-currency debt, depreciations can abruptly render a country insolvent.

Only a handful of the largest economies issue debt denominated in their own currency on international markets, perhaps reflecting in part their economic size and the use of their currencies as a vehicle for international trade. Bonds issued internationally are otherwise relatively homogeneous, usually taking the form of fixed-rate bonds with relatively long maturities. By contrast, the composition of debt issued domestically varies considerably across countries. Few emerging markets issue large amounts of long-term local-currency debt, even in their domestic markets. But a number of them have increasingly made use of domestically issued alternatives to foreign-currency debt, including short-term debt, inflation-indexed debt, and floating-interest-rate debt.

Emerging market countries' difficulties in issuing long-term local-currency bonds on the domestic market seem to result from deeper problems, such as lack of monetary and fiscal policy credibility, and related worries about the possibility of inflation or outright default. While the requisite credibility may take a long time to build, several emerging market countries have recently begun issuing local-currency bonds with maturities of a few years, and have relied on inflation-indexed bonds for longer maturities. Compared with floating-rate and foreign-currency debt, CPI indexation is less likely to lead to debt crises, because it tends to not amplify the effects of adverse shocks. Moreover, the development of domestic private pension funds often creates a natural base of investors seeking the protection against changes in purchasing power that CPI indexation provides.

Regarding debt issued internationally, some international financial institutions (IFIs) have often been among the first parties to issue bonds denominated in the currencies of emerging markets (usually in combination with exchange rate swaps with emerging market residents that issue in one of the world's main currencies). Opportunities to raise funds at more favorable rates have been, and should continue to be, the primary motivation for the IFIs' involvement in these operations: the IFIs have been able to tap new investor bases interested in holding assets denominated in emerging market currencies but bearing no default risk. This said, contributions to the development of new financial markets that can later be tapped by developing countries are a welcome by-product of such funding decisions by the IFIs.

Ideas for Sovereigns from the Corporate Context: Explicit Seniority

Partly as a result of contract enforcement issues, sovereign liability structures both in emerging market countries and in advanced economies are not as rich as those of corporations. A notable difference is a lack of an explicit seniority structure, which at the corporate level exists either by statute or through bond covenants. As a result, sovereign creditors tend to be more exposed to "debt dilution" than do their

---

[7]It is difficult to estimate the extent to which the costs to the domestic economy result from default itself rather than other aspects—such as bank runs or sudden drops in the exchange rate—with which defaults are typically associated. Nevertheless, defaults are associated with widespread bankruptcies, sizable job losses, and declines in domestic demand. In addition, the negative domestic implications of a forced debt restructuring are perceived to be so traumatic that policymakers will delay this option until all other possibilities have been exhausted (IMF, 2002a).

corporate counterparts (Section IV). Debt dilution occurs when new debt reduces the claim that existing creditors can hope to recover in the event of a default. Long recognized as a problem in corporate debt, dilution seems to have recently become a significant problem in emerging sovereign debt markets. For example, by issuing large numbers of new bonds to a wide base of creditors in the 1990s, Argentina drastically reduced the value of the initial bondholders' claims.

Debt dilution has undesirable consequences for both debt structures and the amounts and terms at which sovereigns borrow. Its adverse effects on debt structure stem from investors' efforts to hold debt forms that are harder to dilute—such as short-term debt or debt that is costly to restructure. Such instruments in turn make the debtor more vulnerable to crises and render the impact of crises more severe. Dilution also increases the likelihood that highly indebted countries will overborrow. Countries near default may be able to place new debt with investors without facing prohibitive interest rates, as the new creditors effectively obtain a share of the existing creditors' debt recovery value. At low debt levels, the opposite problem may occur, as the possibility of dilution tends to raise interest rates unnecessarily.

In principle, debt dilution could be ruled out by an explicit, "first-in-time" seniority structure giving priority to earlier debt issues, because in the event of bankruptcy the original creditors would be repaid first. First-in-time seniority would tend to reduce borrowing costs at low debt levels, but make borrowing more expensive at high debt levels. In fact, if the probability of a debt crisis were substantial, markets would expect a new debt issue to be junior to most outstanding debt in the event of a crisis, and thus demand a higher interest rate compared to the present system. The effect on borrowing costs would reward prudent borrowing behavior and discourage overborrowing. Explicit seniority could also improve debt structures by reducing incentives to issue "crisis-prone" debt forms that are hard to dilute.

Explicit seniority would also entail risks, however. In particular, an unavoidable consequence of limiting dilution and making new borrowing harder at high levels of debt is that this may prevent some countries from accessing debt markets in situations of illiquidity, in turn increasing the likelihood of liquidity crises. Another potential drawback is that seniority could complicate debt pricing and, as a result, make debt more expensive (at least until markets became familiar with the new system). Uncertainty would be increased by the possibility that sovereigns find ways to circumvent seniority when their borrowing levels are elevated, for example, by obtaining direct bank loans under different jurisdictions or providing collateral for subsequent loans.

Finally, explicit seniority could have consequences for sovereign debt restructurings, an issue that is not analyzed in this paper.

Explicit seniority in sovereign debt could be implemented in a number of ways, including statutes at the international level; national statutes in debtor countries and issuing jurisdictions; debt contracts; or some combination of the three. This paper explores ideas for a contractual implementation of explicit seniority in general terms and describes some of the obstacles. The two main difficulties that arise in a contractual framework are how to ensure that the sovereign continues to apply the first-in-time seniority structure to all subsequent borrowing and how to enforce the priority structure in the event of restructuring. This paper suggests an approach to deal with those issues, although this area clearly requires further work.

While this paper concludes that explicit seniority is a novel approach to improving debt structures that is worthy of further research, it is only a first pass at the issue, and further research is needed before arriving at a definite conclusion. In fact, while seniority could be beneficial for countries with moderate debt levels, it may make market access more difficult for countries with elevated levels of debt: although desirable in many circumstances to prevent overborrowing, this could present new policy challenges. Moreover, an overall judgment would depend on the effects of seniority on crisis resolution, which is not taken up here. Further analysis would also be needed on how to overcome potential legal and practical obstacles to introducing contract-based seniority. Nevertheless, given the potential benefits of explicit seniority for crisis prevention—and other enhancements to bond contracts that would also mitigate debt dilution—this paper calls for further analysis and discussion of the issue.

Expanding the Set of Instruments: Real Indexation

Another key difference between sovereigns and corporates is that sovereigns lack equity, or equity-like instruments, whereby investors would share in sovereigns' fortunes and misfortunes. Although equity could never be fully reproduced in the sovereign context, the risk-sharing benefits of equity might be mimicked through currently underutilized financial instruments with payment terms indexed to real variables such as gross domestic product (GDP) (Section V).

Real indexation involves higher payments when economic performance is relatively strong, and lower payments when economic performance is relatively weak. For example, countries could issue bonds providing for lower payments when GDP growth is weak or in the event of a natural disaster. Real indexation would thus tend to stabilize the debt-to-GDP ratio, providing two main benefits: first, it would reduce the likelihood of debt crises and, second, it would reduce the need for procyclical fiscal policies.

Indexation to variables largely outside the control of the authorities, such as commodity prices, natural disasters, or output of trading partner countries, might provide considerable insurance benefits, though only to limited groups of countries. Indexation to variables partly within the control of the authorities, such as GDP or exports, could provide substantial insurance benefits to a broad spectrum of countries, though its introduction would present greater challenges.

The cost of such insurance for borrowing countries is likely to depend on the extent to which a number of obstacles can be overcome. In addition to the need for large-scale issuance to ensure market liquidity, the main obstacles seem to relate to the need for investors to be able to hedge the risk involved in holding such instruments; the potential for opportunistic mismeasurement by country authorities of variables partly within their control; and possible difficulties in pricing complex instruments.

The requisite large scale for launching new types of bonds could be attained in the context of a debt restructuring or through international coordination. Should a number of emerging markets issue GDP-indexed bonds, international investors holding a portfolio of such bonds would find GDP risk to be well diversified, because the correlation of growth rates across emerging markets is typically very low. Reforms that would help overcome obstacles related to potential mismeasurement include strengthening the independence of national statistical agencies.

Toward Better Sovereign Debt Structures: A Road Map

Improved debt structures should not be viewed as a substitute for sound policies. Sound policies not only reduce the likelihood of debt crises directly but are also a prerequisite for better debt structures and possible financial innovations that would in turn make countries less prone to crises. Nevertheless, this paper argues that improved debt structures might play a role in ameliorating economic performance and making crises both less likely and less damaging.

Historically, financial innovation seems to have taken place in a somewhat haphazard manner, and has often been prompted by intervention on the part of policymakers (Section VI). Innovations in the areas described above are unlikely to be an exception to this historical norm, especially because the incentives for individual market participants to innovate are likely to be lower than for the group as a whole.

A potential road map for implementing the policy steps analyzed in this paper is likely to require efforts by a number of different actors, including country authorities, international investors, the international community, and researchers.

Sound macroeconomic policies are by far the most important prerequisite for more desirable debt structures. Indeed, excessive reliance on "risky" types of debt is primarily a symptom, rather than a cause, of a perception of risk on the part of investors. Sound policies and credibility are also a precondition for issuing new forms of debt, such as instruments involving elements of real indexation, and for minimizing potentially adverse effects on local banking systems that may be large holders of government debt.

Beyond better policies, country authorities could seek to create or deepen the market for local-currency-denominated debt by issuing, for example, local-currency-denominated bonds with shorter maturities, and inflation-indexed bonds for longer maturities. In doing so, they should be alert to opportunities provided by private pension systems that create a natural demand for local-currency and inflation-indexed debt, and in some cases GDP-indexed debt. In these endeavors, the authorities need to be mindful of sequencing: in countries where long-term local-currency-denominated debt is widely held as a result of restrictions on capital flows or on the range of assets that banks and institutional investors can hold, it would be crucial to establish greater credibility before lifting such restrictions.

There are advantages of using instruments with returns indexed to real variables closely related to issuing countries' economic performance. For those small countries that are especially vulnerable to natural disasters, disaster insurance would seem to be desirable if available at a reasonable cost. Greater use of hedging against commodity price fluctuations would also seem desirable for countries relying on a small set of commodities in their export and revenue structure. Larger, more diversified countries (both advanced and emerging) will be better hedged against macroeconomic fluctuations if they issue bonds indexed to a key macroeconomic aggregate, such as GDP.

Financial market participants' willingness to engage in a dialogue with the official sector, and share their views, expertise, and concerns regarding potential innovations is an indispensable ingredient for progress in improving debt structures. Market participants can only be expected to explore innovations that make good business sense for them. However, two sets of considerations suggest that market participants may collectively have an incentive to participate in such a dialogue. First, the initial costs associated with innovation (including learning costs) are lower when shared by market participants as a group than if incurred individually. Second, innovations—including some in which the official sector played a major role, such as the creation of Brady bonds—have occasionally helped expand the scope of financial markets, thereby generating business opportunities.

The IFIs should continue to track short-term debt and foreign-currency debt as indicators of vulnerability. They should also encourage countries to borrow in local currency and with longer maturities, while recognizing that crisis-prone debt structures typically result from underlying problems that themselves need to be addressed. To the extent that high shares of short-term or foreign-currency debt reflect political economy pressures (perhaps motivated by the electoral calendar) on debt managers to attain short-run interest cost "savings" at the expense of undue increases in the risk of crises, conditionality with respect to debt structure could be considered, on a case-by-case basis. However, its desirability would have to be weighed against the costs that might result, for example, from reducing capital market access for countries where short-term and foreign-currency instruments are the only ways of preserving it—possibly in the context of an incipient liquidity crisis.

While the IFIs' primary goal in deciding upon the currency composition of their own debt issuance must remain the minimization of borrowing costs, market development may continue to be a welcome by-product. The first bond issues in a currency unfamiliar to international markets require substantial additional preparatory work: the IFIs are well placed to work with the authorities toward that end, though the costs in terms of staff resources should not be neglected.

If relatively underutilized instruments such as inflation- or GDP-indexed bonds are deemed desirable, their emergence could be aided in a number of ways: international dialogue among potentially interested parties; strengthened independence of countries' statistical agencies; and technical assistance to improve the quality and transparency of national income statistics.

A number of potential steps analyzed in this paper—such as the creation of an international debt registry to help monitor seniority features of sovereign debt held by private agents—would take somewhat longer to implement. The desirability and practical feasibility of such innovations in the institutional framework could be further explored.

Additional research would seem especially desirable in the following areas:

- the determinants and consequences of domestic debt structures (including the collection of data on domestic debt for a large number of countries);

- empirical evidence on debt dilution and the theoretical case for and against seniority in the sovereign context;

- surveys of investors' and borrowers' attitudes toward financial innovation and obstacles related to it; and

- the development of pricing models for currently underutilized financial instruments.

II Facts on Existing Public Debt Structures

Public debt in emerging market countries differs in several respects from that in advanced economies. First, average debt levels were traditionally equivalent to a lower share of GDP in emerging market countries than they were in advanced economies; the gap has closed in recent years, partly as a result of reductions in the debt of advanced economies (Figure 1). Second, reliance on externally issued debt has been far greater in emerging market countries than in advanced economies. Third, while the structure of external debt of emerging market countries is similar to that of advanced economies, the structure of their domestic debt—in terms of maturity, currency composition, and the prevalence of indexed debt—is very different.[1]

The remainder of the section reviews such differences in greater detail, first, by considering external and domestic debt separately and, second, by offering a consolidated view.

Public Debt in Emerging Market Countries Versus Advanced Economies

Structure of International Debt

The international sovereign debt of emerging market countries consists mainly of medium-term and long-term fixed-interest-rate bonds denominated in foreign currency. Bank loans used to be the main form of financing during the 1970s and 1980s. A stock conversion of loans into bonds took place through the Brady deals; this helps explain the drop in loans, and rise in bonds, in the early 1990s (Figure 2, first panel). When developing countries re-entered international credit markets in the 1990s, they did so mainly through bond issues (Figure 2, second panel). The prevalence of bond financing is not unique to emerging market countries: its relative importance has grown even more sharply in advanced

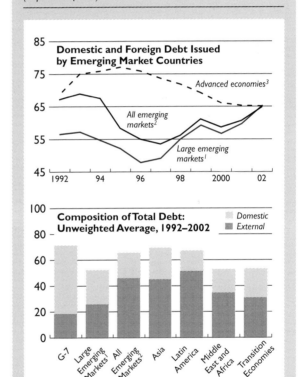

Figure 1. Advanced Economies and Emerging Market Countries: Public Debt Stocks and Debt Composition
(In percent of GDP)

Sources: IMF, *World Economic Outlook* (September 2003); and IMF staff estimates.
[1]Argentina, Brazil, Chile, China, Hungary, India, Indonesia, Israel, Korea, Malaysia, Mexico, Philippines, Poland, Russia, South Africa, Thailand, Turkey, and Venezuela.
[2]Countries listed in footnote 1 above plus Bulgaria, Colombia, Costa Rica, Côte d'Ivoire, Croatia, Ecuador, Egypt, Jordan, Lebanon, Morocco, Nigeria, Pakistan, Panama, Peru, Ukraine, and Uruguay.
[3]Australia, Austria, Belgium, Canada, Denmark, Finland, France, Germany, Greece, Ireland, Italy, Japan, Netherlands, New Zealand, Norway, Portugal, Spain, Sweden, United Kingdom, and United States.

Note: The authors of this section are Marcos Chamon, Olivier Jeanne, and Jeromin Zettelmeyer.

[1]In this paper, "external" (or "international") and "domestic" refer to the jurisdiction where the debt is issued.

Figure 2. Structure of External Public Debt in Emerging Market Countries
(In billions of U.S. dollars)

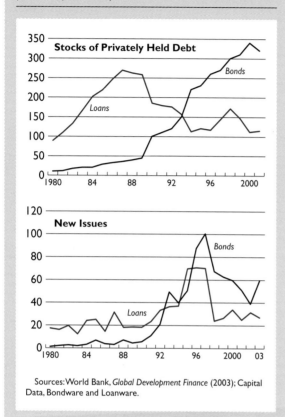

Sources: World Bank, *Global Development Finance* (2003); Capital Data, Bondware and Loanware.

Figure 3. Emerging Market Countries: Fixed- Versus Floating-Rate Sovereign Bond Issues
(In billions of U.S. dollars)

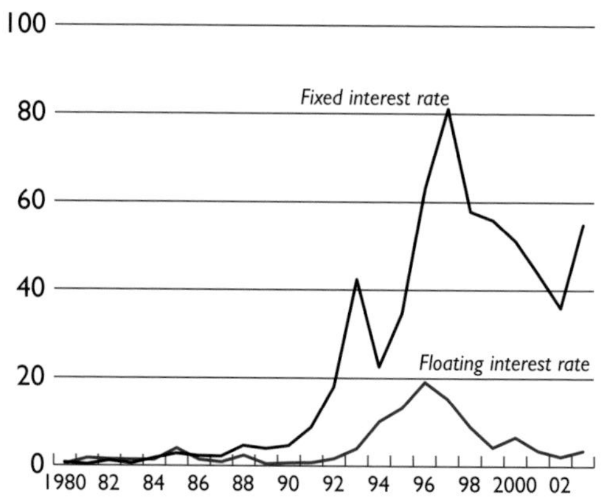

Source: Capital Data, Bondware and Loanware.

economies, where virtually all international borrowing is through bonds.

Most internationally issued public debt carries a fixed interest rate—for both advanced economies and emerging market countries. Much of the emerging market debt issued in the 1970s and 1980s had a floating rate. Certain types of Brady bonds also had a floating rate, and the proportion of floating-rate bonds was relatively high until the mid-1990s: in 1994, about 40 percent of JPMorgan's Emerging Markets Bond Index Global (EMBIG) carried a floating rate. As new bond issues began to take off in the mid-1990s and emerging markets moved from bank loans to bond financing; they also moved from floating-rate to fixed-rate instruments (Figure 3). Currently, floating-rate bonds make up less than 5 percent of the EMBIG.

Most international sovereign debt of emerging market countries is issued at medium-term (5–10 years) or longer-term maturities. However, the average maturity of emerging market countries' debt has declined in recent years, and is now lower than for

advanced economies. The share of the EMBIG consisting of debt with remaining maturities over 20 years declined from 40 percent in the mid-1990s to about 20 percent by the end of 1999, and has stabilized since then (Figure 4, top panel). The decline stems from two factors. First, the 30-year bonds issued through the Brady deals are gradually becoming less important in the stock of emerging market countries' debt as new debt is issued. Second, excluding the Brady bonds, the average maturity of new emerging market countries' bond and loan issues is significantly lower than for advanced economies, and has declined substantially over the past two decades (Figure 4, bottom panel).[2]

Most sovereign debt issued internationally by both emerging market countries and advanced economies is in foreign currency (Table 1). Only a handful of advanced economies issue a substantial share of their international sovereign debt in their own currency. This does not imply that governments in emerging market countries and advanced economies face the same constraints in the international debt market. Indeed, some advanced economies issue local-currency debt in their home markets and attract international investors to purchase it there.

_____

[2]Certain types of short-term debt that have been widely cited as a source of fragility in some recent crises, such as the Mexican Tesobonos in 1994 and the Russian GKOs in 1998, were issued domestically and, hence, were not international debt in the sense used here.

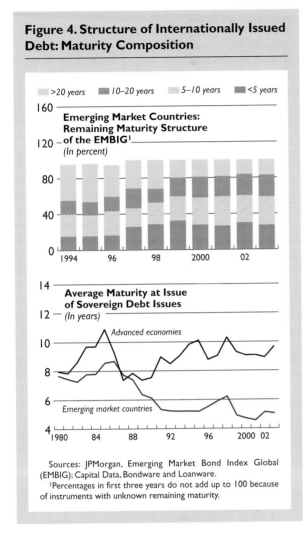

Figure 4. Structure of Internationally Issued Debt: Maturity Composition

Sources: JPMorgan, Emerging Market Bond Index Global (EMBIG); Capital Data, Bondware and Loanware.

[1]Percentages in first three years do not add up to 100 because of instruments with unknown remaining maturity.

Structure of Domestic Debt

The composition of government debt issued on the domestic market is much more heterogeneous across countries than is the composition of debt issued internationally. While there are differences between emerging market countries and advanced economies, these are overwhelmed by differences among emerging markets. On average, emerging market countries rely on long-term local-currency debt to a lesser extent than do advanced economies, but there is substantial variation among emerging markets: such debt is virtually absent in Latin American countries, but represents more than one-half of total debt for several countries in emerging Asia and emerging Europe (Table 2).

More generally, emerging market countries display remarkable differences in terms of the breakdown of domestic government bonds into five categories: local-currency long-term fixed-rate, local-currency

short-term fixed-rate, floating-rate (indexed to a domestic rate), inflation-indexed, and foreign-currency. Each of the first four categories represents more than one-half of total debt in at least one country. There is also significant heterogeneity within regions. In Asia, for example, some issuers (Indonesia and Malaysia) do not make use of long-term local-currency debt whereas other issuers (India, Taiwan Province of China) rely almost exclusively on this form of debt. In Latin America, some countries (Venezuela) borrow mainly through interest-rate-indexed debt, whereas in others (Chile) the majority of government debt is indexed to inflation.

A Consolidated View

Domestic and international debt markets are substitute sources of finance and should be considered jointly. International and domestic debt markets have become integrated, with residents and nonresidents being active in both. For example, in both Argentina and Uruguay, more than half of the international debt was held by residents. Conversely, foreign residents held more than 80 percent of Mexican domestically issued Tesobonos and Cetes before the 1994 crisis (IMF, 1995) and a large share of Russian GKOs and OFZs issued before the 1998 crisis (about 30 percent, according to IMF staff estimates). Sovereigns seem able to choose whether to tap international debt markets or domestic debt markets. In addition to market conditions, this choice depends on two sets of considerations. First, domestic public debt is likely to crowd out financing to the domestic private sector, because some firms may be constrained to the domestic credit market owing to high costs of borrowing abroad. Second, international investors are less protected in domestic jurisdictions.

Obtaining an integrated picture of debt structure that includes both domestic and international debt is difficult owing to data limitations, especially for domestic debt. Since the 1994 Mexican crisis, the international community has made an effort to improve the availability of cross-country statistics.[3] This effort has focused primarily on *external* debt, in spite of the important role played by domestic debt in several recent emerging market crises (Mexico in 1994; Russia in 1998; and Brazil in 1998). Nevertheless, it is possible to establish some basic stylized facts on total (domestic plus international) government debt.

Although advanced economies have traditionally relied on domestic debt markets to a greater extent than have emerging market countries, there seems to have been some convergence in this regard in recent

---

[3]See IMF (2003c).

Table 1. External Sovereign Debt: Currency Composition, 1980–2003[1]
(Unweighted average, in percent)

	Emerging Market Countries[2]	Advanced Economies[3]
Domestic currency[4]	0.3	7.5
Foreign currency	99.7	92.5
U.S. dollar	54.8	42.4
Euro	14.6	6.5
Japanese yen	14.0	14.5
Deutsche mark[5]	11.7	11.1
European Currency Unit (ECU)[5]	. . .	8.0
Others[6]	4.6	10.0

Source: IMF, Bonds, Equities and Loans database.
[1]All bond and loan issues, 1980–2003.
[2]Argentina, Brazil, Chile, China, Hungary, India, Indonesia, Israel, Korea, Malaysia, Mexico, Philippines, Poland, Russia, South Africa, Thailand, Turkey, and Venezuela.
[3]Australia, Austria, Belgium, Canada, Denmark, Finland, France, Germany, Greece, Ireland, Italy, Japan, Netherlands, New Zealand, Norway, Portugal, Spain, Sweden, United Kingdom, and United States.
[4]Includes euro issues (but not European currency unit issues) for European Monetary Union member countries.
[5]Prior to the introduction of the euro.
[6]Includes Italian lira, British pound, French franc, and Swiss franc.

Table 2. Structure of Domestically Issued Government Bonds at End-2001
(In percent of total)

	Domestic Government Bonds/GDP (In percent)	Domestic-Currency-Denominated Bonds				Foreign-Currency-Denominated Bonds
		Not indexed		Indexed to		
		Long term[1]	Short term[1]	Domestic interest rate	Inflation	
Emerging market countries	28.2	41.5	18.6	26.4	7.2	6.3
Latin America	24.0	5.6	13.7	50.8	16.6	13.4
Brazil	52.1	9.5	0.0	53.0	7.0	30.5
Chile[2]	. . .	0.0	21.0	0.0	55.8	23.2
Mexico	11.0	12.8	23.6	60.1	3.5	0.0
Venezuela	9.0	0.0	10.0	90.0	0.0	0.0
Asia	26.6	52.4	16.5	22.2	7.8	1.1
India	27.0	81.6	18.4	0.0	0.0	0.0
Indonesia	34.0	24.6	0.0	30.9	38.9	5.6
Malaysia	36.3	0.0	19.8	80.2	0.0	0.0
Thailand	13.8	91.5	8.5	0.0	0.0	0.0
Philippines	22.0	64.2	35.8	0.0	0.0	0.0
Europe and others	32.4	56.5	23.6	13.6	0.4	5.9
Czech Republic	. . .	41.1	58.9	0.0	0.0	0.0
Hungary	27.0	56.0	23.0	21.0	0.0	0.0
Poland	16.0	62.6	26.5	10.9	0.0	0.0
Slovak Republic	29.0	86.8	13.2	0.0	0.0	0.0
South Africa	35.0	92.4	5.2	0.0	2.4	0.0
Turkey	55.0	0.0	14.5	49.9	0.0	35.6

Sources: IMF staff estimates; and JPMorgan, Guide to Local Markets (2002).
[1]Short term is defined as an initial maturity of less than one year, and long term is defined as an initial maturity of more than one year.
[2]For Chile, the shares refer to bonds issued by the central bank. The amount of bonds issued domestically by the central government is negligible.

years (Figure 5). The domestically issued component of total public debt has increased at a quicker pace than the foreign component in emerging market countries, especially in the 1990s. This may reflect development of the domestic markets, though the increase in total debt also mirrors fiscal expansions.

Nevertheless, much of the increase in domestically issued debt has continued to take the form of foreign-currency debt and short-term debt. The differences between advanced economies and emerging market countries in this respect have thus persisted (Table 3). Consolidating international and domestic debt, about 47 percent of central government debt in emerging market countries was denominated in (or indexed to) a foreign currency in 2001, against about 5 percent for advanced economies. Long-term local-currency debt represented 76 percent of total debt in advanced countries, 36 percent of total debt in emerging market countries, and 15 percent of total debt in Latin America. While inflation-indexed public debt issues have been at the forefront of the development of domestic debt markets in a few countries, foreign-currency issues have been key in most others.

Figure 5. Emerging Market Countries: Structure of Public Debt
(In percent of GDP)

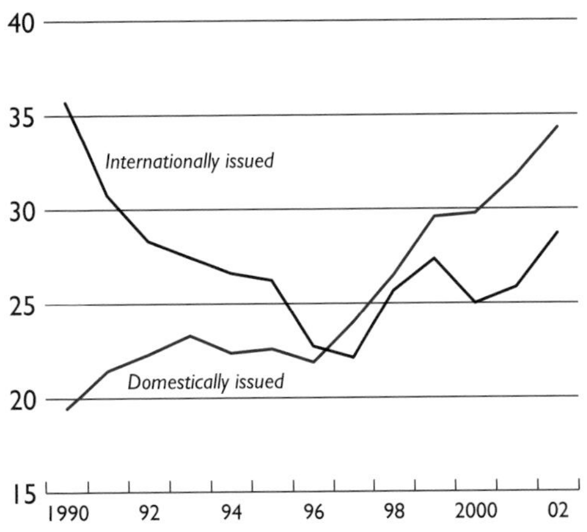

Source: IMF staff estimates.

Sovereign Versus Corporate Liability Structures

Moving to a comparison between sovereigns and corporates, the richer liability structure of corporates is apparent along three dimensions. First, and by far the most striking, a large share of corporate liabilities consists of outside equity.[4] Moreover, corporates make use of financial instruments that combine debt and equity, such as convertible bonds—the holder can convert these bonds into stocks at a predetermined exchange ratio at prespecified dates. In contrast, sovereigns lack not only equity but also equity-like instruments that would make returns a direct function of variables such as tax revenues, the fiscal balance, or GDP.[5] Second, corporations make extensive use of collateralized (secured) debt as well as seniority distinctions within unsecured debt. In contrast, sovereigns issue comparatively little secured debt, and unsecured debt is not formally prioritized. Third, corporate bond contracts sometimes include

covenants that place restrictions on future financing decisions of the firm, by placing limits on total indebtedness, or restricting the issuance of debt at the same or higher levels of seniority. No such restrictions exist at the sovereign level, at least in debt contracts with private creditors.[6]

Use of Secured and Subordinated Debt

Corporations in advanced economies typically issue liabilities belonging to several classes with different priority in the event of liquidation or bankruptcy reorganization. These include secured debt,[7] ordinary unsecured debt, subordinated debt, preferred stock, and common stock. Secured debt gives the title to a pledged asset to the debtor. The remaining liability classes define an absolute priority ranking: in the event of liquidation, each of them is to be repaid only if the higher ranking class was repaid in full.[8] Both

---

[4]In a sample of 5,000 U.S. industrial corporations surveyed by Barclay and Smith (1995), the average ratio between debt and common stock was about 1 in 3, that is, common stock made up about 75 percent of total firm value on average.

[5]Informally speaking, a country's currency might be viewed as having a few of the features of equity. Investors holding currency, or other local-currency-denominated assets, share in the fortunes of the issuing country: as the real exchange rate is correlated with economic performance, real returns tend to be higher when the country's economic growth is relatively strong.

---

[6]IMF programs typically restrict total nonconcessional debt (see below in this section).

[7]Including capital leases, in which the contract promises a fixed payments stream, and the leased capital asset can be seized (repossessed) by the creditor in the event of default.

[8]In U.S. bankruptcy reorganizations under Chapter 11, absolute priority is frequently violated: equity holders often receive securities of positive market value even though some debt holders are not fully repaid (Franks and Torous, 1989; Weiss, 1990). However, deviations from absolute priority *among* debt holders seem to be rare.

Table 3. Structure of Total (Domestic and External) Central Government Debt, 2001
(In percent of total)

	Foreign-Currency Debt[1]	Long-Term Domestic-Currency Debt[1]	Total Debt as a Share of GDP (In percent)
Emerging market countries	47.1	35.7	48.8
Latin America	67.9	15.2	37.0
Argentina	96.8	...	53.7
Brazil	43.8[2]	3.3[3,4]	66.2[2,5]
Chile	92.7	0.0	15.6
Mexico	35.6	57.5[6]	22.6
Venezuela	70.6	0.0	27.0
Asia	29.3	53.7	56.5
China	17.7	82.3	24.0
India	14.5	69.9[7]	65.1[7]
Indonesia	46.0	51.0[6]	90.9
Malaysia	16.7	0.0	69.2
Philippines	47.4	17.6[8]	64.9
Thailand	33.6	78.8	24.8
Others	47.6	17.4	51.3
Poland	34.8	34.8	39.3
Russia	90.3	...	50.0
South Africa	14.4	61.2[3,4,8]	46.8
Hungary	30.1	44.0[9]	52.1
Turkey	68.2	0.0	68.5
Advanced economies[6]	5.6	75.9	51.8
Australia	0.5[3]	85.5[3]	10.1
Belgium	1.3	80.4	101.2
Canada	6.0[3]	41.5[3]	40.3
Denmark	12.1	69.0	52.5
Finland	16.3	66.7	45.4
France	0.0	92.0	49.4
Germany	0.0	97.0	35.3
Italy	3.2	86.8	102.6
Japan	0.0	74.8	121.6
Netherlands	0.0	81.0	43.1
New Zealand	18.5[3]	48.2[3]	31.2
Norway	3.7[3]	60.5[3]	18.4
Portugal	8.6	87.4	58.9
Spain	4.1[3]	83.8[3]	47.2
Sweden	20.1	55.9	51.6
United Kingdom	1.4	60.5	38.6
United States	0.0	58.8	33.1

Sources: IMF staff; OECD, *Central Government Debt Yearbook 1992–2001*; and websites of the country authorities.
[1]In percent of total central government debt for emerging market countries and total central government marketable debt for advanced economies.
[2]Includes debt held by the Central Bank.
[3]Based on residual maturity.
[4]Only marketable domestic-currency bonds.
[5]Consolidated government debt.
[6]Includes debt indexed to inflation and domestic interest rates.
[7]Includes debt owed to National Small Savings Funds.
[8]Includes debt with maturities of three years or more.
[9]Data for 2002.

secured and subordinated debt make up significant portions of the corporate debt stock.[9]

In contrast, sovereign liabilities generally fall into just two classes—secured debt and unsecured debt. Within the unsecured debt class, there is no distinction between ordinary debt and subordinated debt. Secured sovereign claims are generally collateralized by future receipts, such as oil revenue or other export receivables (Chalk, 2002; and IMF, 2003d). To serve as collateral, future receipts need to be removed from the direct control of the sovereign, that is, the transactions associated with future receipts need to occur under foreign jurisdiction. For this reason, collateralized future receipts typically involve export revenues accruing to the government (usually through a public enterprise), rather than domestic tax revenues.

Secured debt is a far smaller proportion of total debt for sovereigns than it is for corporations. Of the 79 developing and emerging market countries that had at least one public sector (including public enterprises) international loan or bond outstanding on January 1, 2003, about half (39 countries) owed collateralized loans or bonds. However, the face value of collateralized debt was only 6.2 percent of the face value of total debt outstanding (7.1 percent in the group of countries that had some collateralized debt). The share of collateralized loans or bonds in total loans and bonds was higher than 25 percent in only 9 countries. In the postwar era, secured sovereign debt is a relatively recent phenomenon: the first modern collateralized bond was issued by Mexico in 1988 (Figure 6).[10]

Financing Restrictions in Debt Contracts

Corporate bond contracts in the United States have often contained "negative covenants" that restrict fu-

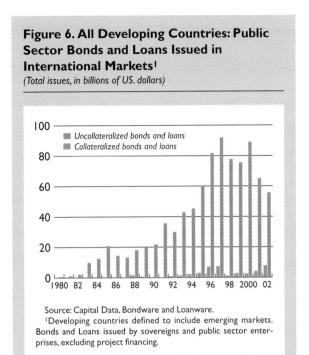

Figure 6. All Developing Countries: Public Sector Bonds and Loans Issued in International Markets[1]
(Total issues, in billions of US. dollars)

Source: Capital Data, Bondware and Loanware.
[1]Developing countries defined to include emerging markets. Bonds and Loans issued by sovereigns and public sector enterprises, excluding project financing.

ture financing decisions (Smith and Warner, 1979; Asquith and Wizman, 1990; and Goyal, 2003). These include clauses that place restrictions on net worth or total debt, possibly excepting subordinated debt. These clauses protect creditors from dilution through additional debt issued in the same seniority class (see Section IV). Creditor protections of this type—in particular, restrictions on future debt issues—are generally absent from sovereign debt.[11]

Some elements of IFI conditionality could be interpreted as analogous to negative covenants, in the sense that—among other purposes—they serve to protect the financial interests of IFI creditors by restricting the borrower's financing decisions (e.g., by limiting the fiscal deficit or placing limits on external debt). Analogous conditions or covenants do not exist in privately held debt.

---

[9]Secured debt constituted 53 percent of the debt of the average U.S. industrial firm (38 percent if leases are excluded), ordinary debt 35 percent, and subordinated debt 12 percent (Barclay and Smith, 1995). Large firms tend to issue more ordinary and subordinated debt, whereas smaller firms tend to issue more secured debt. About 75 percent of firms issued liabilities in at least three priority classes, that is, common stock plus at least two debt classes (or preferred stock and at least one debt class). The results are similar for the United Kingdom (Lasfer, 1999).

[10]Sovereigns made greater use of collateralized bonds in the pre–World War I era. Collateral usually took the form of infrastructure (especially railways), raw materials, or, especially when bonds were issued following a debt restructuring, tax revenues (Mauro and Yafeh, 2003).

---

[11]The main exception is the "negative pledge clause" in sovereign bond contracts and official debt, which prohibits new collateralized debt unless the incumbent debt holders are given an equal claim on the collateral.

III   Rendering Debt Structures Less Crisis Prone with Existing Instruments

Existing debt structures in emerging market countries seem to rely excessively on risky forms of debt—such as short-term and foreign-currency debt—which may amplify the economic cycle, increase the likelihood of crises, and make crises more difficult to manage. Increases in risky forms of debt may be the result of worsening debt sustainability, but they also reinforce the rise in vulnerability.

Problems with the Status Quo

Short-Term Debt

Empirical studies have found short-term debt to be a leading indicator of vulnerability to international financial crises (Bussière and Mulder, 1999; and Rodrik and Velasco, 1999). Theoretical models have put forward two types of mechanisms to explain this empirical association.

First, short-term debt may make governments more vulnerable to debt rollover crises. Indeed, this seems to have been an important factor in triggering the recent crises in Mexico (1994) and Russia (1998). In the extreme case of a pure liquidity crisis, investors stop lending to the government simply because they expect others to do the same. If the average maturity of the debt is low, the government is then at the mercy of self-fulfilling creditor panics that can be triggered by shifts in market sentiment (Sachs, 1984; Alesina, Prati, and Tabellini, 1990; Cole and Kehoe, 2000; and Chamon, 2003). In the less extreme but probably more realistic case where the crisis mixes elements of illiquidity and insolvency, the government would be vulnerable to a piece of bad news, whose real impact would be amplified by creditors' unwillingness to roll over their claims (Jeanne, 2004; in the corporate context, see Diamond, 1991).

Second, short-term debt can give rise to vicious circles stemming from the two-way interaction between debt levels and interest rates. If the debt has a short maturity or bears a floating interest rate, changes not only in the international interest rates but also in the country's own creditworthiness will affect the interest bill relatively quickly. A sovereign with a high level of short-term debt may thus find itself trapped in a bad equilibrium in which high interest payments lead to a high probability of default, which in turn increases the default risk premium and the interest rate (Calvo, 1988).

More generally, the relatively short average maturity of debt in emerging markets may also amplify the economic cycle. In emerging market countries, economic downturns are typically associated with increases in interest rates because of increases in the default and devaluation risk premiums, thus reducing the scope for countercyclical fiscal policies.[1]

Foreign-Currency Debt

The vulnerabilities created by significant levels of debt denominated in (or indexed to) a foreign currency have also been evident in several recent crises, an aspect emphasized, for both private and public debt, in the balance sheet approach to crises (Allen and others, 2002). In fact, the depreciation of the local currency has often led to a sharp increase in government debt as a share of domestic GDP or fiscal receipts (Figure 7). The contribution of this revaluation was especially large in Argentina and Uruguay—two countries where the fraction of debt denominated in foreign currency and the depreciation of the local currency were substantial. By contrast, it was small in Korea, where the government had little foreign-currency debt, and in Turkey, where the real depreciation of the currency was moderate.

Not only does foreign-currency debt make crises more severe but it also reduces the scope for domestic policies to alleviate the impact of crises. The

Note: The authors of this section are Marcos Chamon and Olivier Jeanne.

[1]GDP growth is negatively correlated with the spread on foreign-currency bonds issued internationally by emerging market countries (Eichengreen and Mody, 1998). This effect is likely augmented, for domestic currency borrowing, by the expected depreciation premium.

revaluation of government debt amplifies the initial fiscal problem and reduces the ability of the government to implement policies that might mitigate the disruption in the private sector (Jeanne and Zettelmeyer, 2002). In addition, monetary policy cannot be used to inflate foreign-currency debt away. The government is faced with the well-known and much-debated dilemma of choosing between raising the interest rate and letting the currency depreciate, with both options having adverse effects on domestic balance sheets.

Such amplification mechanisms resulting from high shares of foreign-currency debt create the potential for vicious circles and can thus make countries more vulnerable to crises in the first place. Imbalances in domestic balance sheets would lead investors to attack the local currency; with the resulting depreciation, balance sheets would in turn deteriorate even further (Krugman, 1999; Aghion, Bacchetta, and Banerjee, 2001; and Jeanne and Zettelmeyer, 2002).

Determinants of Government Debt Structure

Why do governments in emerging market countries and their lenders settle on debt that seems to be unduly crisis prone, even though they are the first ones to suffer the costs in a crisis? Lack of credibility of monetary and fiscal policies seems to be an important factor. Other factors may also be at work, including the nature of the domestic investor base and characteristics of domestic financial regulation (in the case of domestic debt), as well as the country's economic size (in the case of international debt).

Credibility of Monetary and Fiscal Policies

Governments in many emerging market countries cannot borrow on the same terms as advanced economies because of lack of credibility of monetary and fiscal policies. Unsustainable policies lead creditors to anticipate that the government will expropriate them in one way or another—directly through a default or indirectly through inflation if debt is denominated in local currency. Thus, not only do governments face higher and more volatile interest rates, and—from time to time—loss of market access, but they are also under pressure to issue debt instruments that are more prone to crises.

Lack of credibility plays an especially important role in the period leading up to crises, as governments tend to shift the composition of their debt toward shorter maturities and foreign-currency denomination. Notable examples include Mexico's shift to Tesobonos in 1994 and Brazil's switch to-

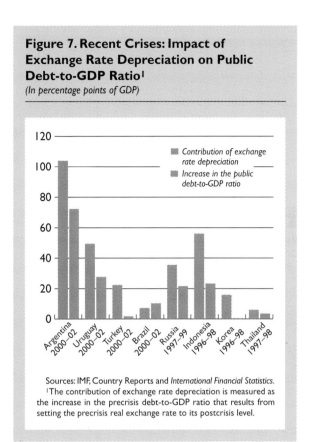

Figure 7. Recent Crises: Impact of Exchange Rate Depreciation on Public Debt-to-GDP Ratio[1]
(In percentage points of GDP)

- Contribution of exchange rate depreciation
- Increase in the public debt-to-GDP ratio

Sources: IMF, Country Reports and *International Financial Statistics.*
[1]The contribution of exchange rate depreciation is measured as the increase in the precrisis debt-to-GDP ratio that results from setting the precrisis real exchange rate to its postcrisis level.

ward short-term, foreign-currency, and floating-rate debt in 1998.[2] These examples are consistent with the view that short-term debt is a symptom, rather than a cause, of an impending crisis.[3] With a looming crisis, investors would usually prefer to hold short-term debt for two reasons:

- *Dilution.* First, investors holding short-term debt may expect the government to repay them before the default actually takes place (Rogoff, 1999). Thus issuing short-term debt dilutes the outstanding long-term debt.[4]

[2]In the period leading up to Mexico's 1994 crisis, both the stock of Tesobonos and the interest rate differential between the peso-denominated Cetes and the dollar-linked Tesobonos rose sharply (IMF, 1995, pp. 53–69, Figures I–6 and I–7).

[3]Indeed, systematic panel regressions show that, while higher shares of short-term debt are associated with greater likelihood of debt crises, that association is no longer significant when taking into account that greater use of short-term debt is itself influenced by other factors, including low credibility (Detragiache and Spilimbergo, 2001).

[4]Anticipating dilution, investors could be reluctant to lend on a long-term basis or be willing to do so only at high interest rates (Bolton and Jeanne, 2004). In fact, the government could use short-term debt to postpone the necessary adjustment at the expense of long-term creditors. However, such dilution might turn out to be desirable, even for long-term creditors, if it bought time to permit the necessary adjustment and avoided a default.

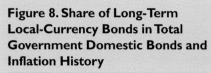

Figure 8. Share of Long-Term Local-Currency Bonds in Total Government Domestic Bonds and Inflation History

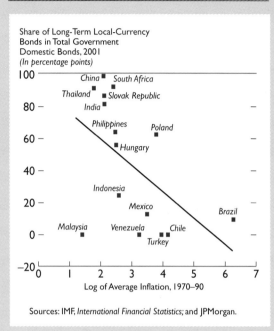

Share of Long-Term Local-Currency Bonds in Total Government Domestic Bonds, 2001
(In percentage points)

Sources: IMF, *International Financial Statistics*; and JPMorgan.

not prove that they can be trusted with long-term local-currency debt because of creditors' fears that such debt would be inflated away (Jeanne, 2003). Second, private agents may get used to a certain type of instrument, and impediments to financial innovation may hamper the transition to a different financial structure.

The prevalence of foreign-currency or inflation-indexed debt may be the result of past disinflation and fiscal stabilization efforts. When inflation is high because of an underlying fiscal problem, the authorities may be caught in a vicious circle in which inflationary expectations imply high interest rates on local-currency debt; in turn these make it more difficult to stabilize the fiscal and monetary situation (Calvo, 1988). The government can seek to break such vicious circles by borrowing in foreign currency, or with indexed debt, at lower interest rates. If a lower interest rate is not sufficient to make the debt dynamics sustainable, and a fiscal adjustment is required, foreign-currency debt and inflation-indexed debt can make the government's commitment to the adjustment more credible, because they cannot be inflated away (Calvo and Guidotti, 1990).

A relatively large share of foreign-currency or indexed debt may result from investors' and borrowers' attempts to protect themselves from uncertainty in an environment of high and variable inflation (Ize and Parrado, 2002). With long-term domestic-currency debt, the future real burden of debt is very uncertain at the time of issue, and could be unsustainably high if inflation turns out to be much lower than expected. This risk is especially relevant for countries with an imperfectly credible fixed exchange rate peg and high domestic interest rates. Borrowing at a high interest rate in domestic currency effectively involves a bet that the currency will be devalued—a bet that can turn out to be very costly in the event the devaluation does not occur. In such an environment, foreign-currency debt, CPI-indexed debt, or floating-rate debt may be less risky than long-term local-currency debt (Jeanne, 2003).

From the point of view of borrowing countries, the relative desirability of local-currency debt, foreign-currency debt, and CPI-indexed debt can be assessed by looking at the unit in which domestic output is the most stable (Box 1). For most emerging markets, relatively volatile inflation implies that GDP is far more stable when expressed in foreign-currency terms than in local-currency terms. (The opposite holds for the G-7 countries; see also Fontenay, Milesi-Ferretti, and Pill, 1997; and Missale, 1999.) Thus a simple hedging motive may help explain the greater reliance on foreign-currency debt in emerging market countries. Interestingly, for both the G-7 and emerging mar-

• *Discipline.* Second, investors may expect that if the government deviated from desirable policies, it would soon face higher interest rates or a roll-over crisis (Diamond, 1993; Diamond and Rajan, 2001; and Jeanne, 2004). Short-term debt may be the best option when the need for discipline outweighs the expected costs—to both the borrower and its lenders—resulting from the possibility of a rollover crisis.

High-inflation episodes durably change the structure of government debt. Indeed, no country that has experienced hyperinflation has a significant fraction of its government debt in long-term local-currency instruments (Table 3). Furthermore, in an admittedly limited cross section of countries for which data are available, the average inflation rate in 1970–90 is negatively associated with the share of long-term local-currency instruments in government domestic debt in 2001 (Figure 8; Jeanne, 2003).

The persistence of foreign-currency and indexed debt—in some cases long after disinflation or fiscal adjustment have been achieved—may reflect two factors. First, it often takes decades for countries to gain anti-inflationary credibility: some countries may even be trapped in a situation where they can-

Box 1. Debt Structure and Hedging

In assessing the relative merits of local-currency debt, foreign-currency debt, and inflation-indexed debt, a key criterion is which type of debt results in the lowest probability of the debt-to-GDP ratio exceeding a given threshold. This is equivalent to asking whether the volatility of output is lowest when output is expressed in terms of local currency, dollars, or the consumer price index. In fact, debt commits the borrower to repay a fixed quantity in terms of some unit—the local currency, a foreign currency, or, for inflation-indexed debt, a price index. For example, a 10-year dollar-denominated zero coupon bond issued in 2004 commits the government to repay a certain quantity $D^\$$ of dollars in 2014. Assuming that this is the only debt issued by the government, the debt-to-GDP ratio in 2014 is given by $D^\$/Y^\$$, where $Y^\$$ is the country's GDP in 2014 *expressed in terms of dollars*. Viewed from 2004, the principal debt repayment due is known (with no uncertainty): the likelihood that the debt-to-

GDP ratio will exceed a given threshold is therefore entirely determined by the volatility of $Y^\$$. More generally, debt denominated in unit A is preferable to debt denominated in unit B if output is less variable when expressed in unit A than in unit B. Thus one way of assessing the relative desirability of local-currency debt, dollar debt, and CPI-indexed debt is simply to compare the volatility of output expressed in terms of local currency, dollars, and the consumer price index. In the exercise conducted below, volatility is defined more precisely as the standard deviation of those changes in the 10-year growth rate of output (in each of the three units, considered in turn) that cannot be predicted on the basis of past output growth. For advanced economies, or G-7 countries, the volatility of output is lower when denominated in local currency than it is when denominated in foreign currency, but for emerging market countries, this is reversed, owing to their higher and more volatile inflation.

Standard Deviation of Cumulative 10-Year Unexpected Growth
(In percentage points)

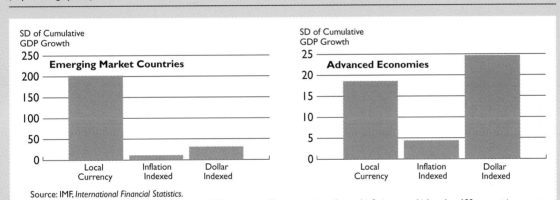

Source: IMF, *International Financial Statistics.*

Note: The sample of emerging markets consists of 11 countries. (None experienced annual inflation rates higher than 100 percent in any year during 1955–2000). The result that GDP is more stable when expressed in foreign-currency terms rather than in local-currency terms becomes even more striking when countries that experienced inflation rates above 100 percent are included in the sample. The sample of advanced economies consists of 21 countries. Unexpected output growth is the difference between actual growth and the growth predicted by an autoregressive (AR (1)) process. The sample period is 1965–2000. For a given year, growth is predicted for the subsequent 10 years based on data for the previous 20 years.

ket countries, the volatility of GDP is smallest when GDP is expressed in terms of CPI-indexed units, suggesting that CPI-indexed bonds may provide substantial advantages to both groups of countries.

Finally, governments may borrow in foreign currency to reduce nominal interest payments (which are high in local-currency terms owing to the inflation premium) and thus the headline fiscal deficit (Blejer and Cheasty, 1991). Typical measures of

the public deficit take into account the flow of interest payments but not the changes in the real value of the principal due to currency depreciation or inflation.[5]

---

[5]Several countries where inflation is an important consideration report an "operational" fiscal balance that includes the effect of inflation on the debt principal.

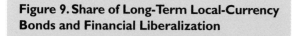

Figure 9. Share of Long-Term Local-Currency Bonds and Financial Liberalization

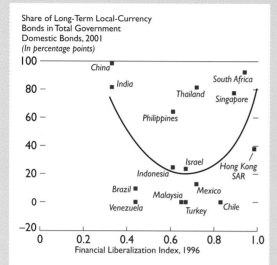

Share of Long-Term Local-Currency
Bonds in Total Government
Domestic Bonds, 2001
(In percentage points)

Sources: Abiad and Mody (2003); IMF, *International Financial Statistics;* and JPMorgan.
Note: The financial liberalization index refers to 1996: the latest available from Abiad and Mody (2003). Although the quadratic term in the regression corresponding to the figure is statistically significant, the small number of observations suggests the U-Shape shown above should be interpreted as merely suggestive.

Domestic Investor Base, Financial Regulation, and Pension Systems

A large base of domestic investors may be expected to make it easier for a country to absorb shocks to capital flows and, more specifically, for the government to issue debt domestically and in local currency, if this is not precluded by a history of high inflation (IMF, 2003e). Indeed, countries with a larger domestic investor base—as proxied by the ratio of bank deposits to GDP—are found to have a smaller share of foreign-currency bonds in total (private and public) bonds (Claessens, Klingebiel, and Schmukler, 2003). The type of pension system has important consequences for the size of the domestic investor base, and thus the development of the domestic government debt market. Prefunded pension systems are likely to induce significant domestic savings available for investment in government domestic debt, though in practice the relationship between pension systems and the share of domestic debt is not straightforward, probably because of the presence of other determinants of debt structure.

Governments may also create a captive market for their debt—including long-term debt—through financial regulation, moral suasion, or direct control of

financial institutions. Many countries have regulations that prevent domestic pension funds from investing more than a fraction of their portfolios in foreign assets: such regulations can be quite constraining, even in the case of OECD countries (Fischer and Reisen, 1994). Moreover, in financially repressed countries, the government may induce domestic banks to buy its debt, especially where the government controls a large share of the banking system. Finally, the presence of capital controls has been found to be associated with the share of local-currency borrowing in the domestic credit market (Hausmann and Panizza, 2002).

Indeed, the share of long-term local-currency instruments in total government domestic debt is high not only in financially liberalized countries with relatively strong policy credibility, such as many advanced economies, but also in countries with lower degrees of financial liberalization (Figure 9). This may be tentatively interpreted in terms of three stages in the development of domestic government debt markets. In a first stage, in some developing countries, financial repression forces residents to hold long-term nominal local-currency debt. As countries develop and move to a second stage, however, they often ease restrictions even before establishing strong credibility: investors thus may shift to other forms of debt. In a third stage, countries attain credibility while refraining from restrictions, and investors hold long-term local-currency debt voluntarily, as in advanced economies.

Political Economy Determinants

The determinants of government domestic debt structures are rooted in the domestic political economy. Explanations under the heading of "lack of policy credibility" are ultimately related to different ways in which the government can reduce the burden of its obligations to creditors. The risk of nonpayment is in turn determined by the stability of the government and the weight that creditors carry in the political arena. Great Britain in the seventeenth century is an especially interesting example, because it was the first country to develop a government debt market comparable in size to those observed now in advanced economies. It has been argued that this was made possible by the new system of checks and balances set up after the Glorious Revolution, which gave creditors more control over the government (North and Weingast, 1989). A domestic creditor constituency may also help ensure that the government will respect creditor rights.

Political economy considerations have some implications for the link between financial repression and the development of the domestic debt market. Even if long-term nominal debt were the result of financial repression, this would not necessarily imply that the government would seek to expropriate its creditors. Defaulting on a debt that is held by domestic banks would likely generate a financial meltdown. Thus, the government's incentives to avoid a default are likely greater if domestic banks hold the public debt.

Measures of political stability and rule of law are positively correlated with the domestic public debt as a share of GDP (Figure 10). This is consistent with previous findings of a significant correlation between the size of the domestic local-currency bond market (including both private and public debt) and political economy variables, such as rule of law and democracy (Burger and Warnock, 2003; and Claessens, Klingebiel, and Schmukler, 2003).

Finally, historical accidents may contribute to explaining the development of domestic debt markets in local currency: changes in financial structure that occurred because of a transitory event often persist long after the event. For example, Canada and Australia developed their domestic long-term local-currency debt market during World War I because the government had large financing needs that could no longer be fulfilled by borrowing on London's financial markets (Bordo, Meissner, and Reddish, 2003).

International Debt Market

It has been argued that many countries, both emerging and advanced, are unable to issue in their own currency on international markets at reasonable cost, owing to an unwillingness of international investors to bear exchange rate risk. In existing empirical studies, issuance of bonds in local currency is not found to be closely related to countries' policies or institutions (Hausmann and Panizza, 2002). Nor do these variables seem to help explain the (admittedly limited) variation across countries in the structure of sovereign debt issued on international markets. However, countries' economic size seems to be associated with whether they issue bonds in their own currency on international markets. This is suggested by both systematic cross-country regressions on modern data (Eichengreen, Hausmann, and Panizza, 2002) and historical evidence. In the nineteenth century, for example, local-currency debt issued by a few "emerging markets" of the time, such as Russia, was actively traded on the secondary market in London (Flandreau and Sussman, 2002). By contrast, the local-currency debt of countries judged to have better creditworthiness, such as the Nordic countries, was not traded in London. The role of the ruble as a vehicle currency for a large number of international trade and finance transactions may help explain this difference.

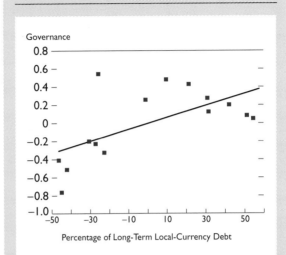

Figure 10. Institutional Quality and Domestically Issued Long-Term Local-Currency Debt
(Component orthogonal to per capita GDP)

Sources: JPMorgan, *Guide to Emerging Markets* (2001); and Kaufmann, Kraay, and Mastruzzi (2003).

Note: The scatter plot shows the association between an indicator of governance and the size of the local-currency debt market, taking into account that both these variables are associated with GDP per capita. The horizontal axis reports the residuals of a regression of long-term local-currency debt on GDP per capita. The vertical axis reports the residuals of a regression of an institutional index on GDP per capita. The correlation is significant at the 5 percent level. The correlation between governance and the share of long-term local-currency is highly significant when not controlling for GDP per capita.

Policy Implications

Domestic Debt Markets

To make public debt structures less crisis prone, a key long-term policy objective is to develop a deep domestic market for government debt, especially for long-term local-currency instruments. Issuing long-term local-currency debt requires monetary and fiscal credibility. In part, this can be gained through a combination of policy success—such as stabilizing from high inflation and reducing public debt levels—and institutional reforms that create an expectation that stabilization gains will be sustained. The latter include medium-term fiscal and monetary policy frameworks that constrain future policy choices, such as longer-term fiscal and inflation targets, and central bank independence. In the long run, such institutions may be a better foundation for policy credibility than the discipline that comes from risky forms of debt (Falcetti and Missale, 2002).

Box 2. Creating Domestic Markets for Long-Term Domestic-Currency Bonds: Country Experiences

A number of emerging markets—including Colombia, India, Singapore, South Africa, Taiwan Province of China, and Thailand—have traditionally issued long-term domestic debt in local currency. This reflects long histories of low or moderate inflation, in some cases combined with financial repression. Recently, however, some countries have begun to issue long-term, nonindexed local-currency debt, in spite of having experienced high inflation during the 1970s or 1980s, and liberalizing their capital markets.

Chile last experienced high inflation in the 1970s and inflation has remained moderate since the early 1980s. Until recently, more than half of the public debt was inflation indexed, reflecting a desire to promote indexation as a way of avoiding dollarization, and to conduct monetary policy in terms of "real" policy rates and a "real" term structure of interest rates. As part of that strategy, indexed bonds of 8–20-year maturity were issued in the early 1990s. With inflation in the low single-digit levels (since 1999) and the adoption of a formal inflation targeting regime, the policy interest rate switched to nominal targets (August 2001). Subsequently, the central bank issued two-year and five-year nonindexed peso bonds.

Israel stabilized from high inflation in 1985. Inflation initially fell to moderate levels (10–20 percent) and later—after 1995—to single digits. In 1985, about 40 percent of public sector debt was in foreign currency, while the rest was inflation-indexed local-currency debt. By 2002, foreign-currency debt had disappeared, the share of inflation-indexed debt was less than 40 percent, and nonindexed local-currency debt made up the remaining debt stock. This transformation took place in two stages. First, foreign-currency debt was reduced and substituted by inflation-indexed debt, which peaked at 80 percent in the 1990s. Second, inflation-indexed debt was gradually substituted by nonindexed local-currency debt. A two-year nonindexed bond was first introduced in 1995. Subsequently,

the maturities of local-currency bonds were gradually lengthened: 5-year, 7-year, and 10-year bonds were introduced in 1998, 2000, and 2001, respectively. Average maturity in 2002 stood at about six years.

Mexico had its last high inflation episode in 1987–88. Inflation fell to single-digit levels by 1993–94, rose to moderate levels after the 1994–95 crisis, and fell again to single-digit levels by 2000. In the decade between 1989 and 1999, domestic debt consisted mainly of short-term local-currency debt and floating-rate debt—except for the well-known sharp increase in short-term foreign-currency debt leading up to the 1994 crisis—with inflation-indexed debt generally taking a third place. This began to change in 2000, when the Mexican government issued 3-year and 5-year nonindexed bonds, followed by 7-year and 10-year bonds in 2002, and, finally, a 20-year bond in 2003.

Poland stabilized from near-hyperinflationary levels in 1991. Inflation hovered at about 30 percent until 1996, then dropped to 10–20 percent and finally (in 1999) to single-digit levels. Until 1992, all of Poland's local-currency debt, which was small relative to its foreign-currency debt, consisted of short-term treasury bills. In 1992, Poland introduced an inflation-indexed one-year bond and a three-year floating-rate bond. In 1994—with inflation still at around 30 percent—2-year and 5-year nonindexed local-currency bonds were introduced, followed by a 10-year floating-rate bond in 1995, and a 10-year nonindexed bond in 1999. The share of foreign-currency debt in domestic debt fell from about 20 percent in 1994 to essentially zero in 2002.

These experiences share a common pattern. Nonindexed bonds of more than five-year maturity were issued almost immediately after fiscal stabilization, the decline of inflation to low single-digit levels, and the adoption of formal inflation-targeting regimes (Israel in 1991; Chile, Poland, and Mexico in 1999) and formal central bank independence (Chile in 1989; Mexico in 1994; Poland in 1998). Moreover, all countries undertook major pension reforms in the direction of fully funded systems. This suggests that the development of a long-term local-currency bond market requires substantial and credible reforms but is feasible without a long period of credibility building.

Sources: Galindo and Leiderman (2003); Herrera and Valdés (2003); Werner (2003); IMF Country Reports; and national statistical sources.

It has been argued that, even with stabilization and institutional reforms, acquiring sufficient credibility to issue long-term local-currency debt may take several years or even decades (Caballero, Cowan, and Kearns, 2003, based on a comparison between Australia and Chile). However, a number of countries have recently been able to issue nonindexed long-term debt almost immediately after stabilizing at low

levels of inflation and reforming their monetary policy frameworks (Box 2). In addition, governments that are unable to issue nonindexed long-term debt can become less reliant on risky debt forms by issuing inflation-indexed debt.

The main advantage of inflation-indexed debt is that it breaks the automatic link between government solvency and large exchange rate swings that

---

Box 3. Developing International Markets for Bonds in Emerging Market Currencies

A considerable share of the relatively rare international bonds denominated in emerging market currencies have not been issued by sovereigns, but rather by international organizations or multinational corporations that were able to reduce their borrowing costs by issuing in those emerging market currencies and, when they did not have a natural hedge, engaging in currency swaps. This process began in the mid-1980s with the currencies of countries such as Italy, Portugal, and Spain and in recent years has involved the currencies of emerging market countries such as Brazil, Chile, the Czech Republic, Hungary, Mexico, Poland, the Slovak Republic, and South Africa. Such opportunities for savings may be the result of the ability to tap an investor base that seeks to hold bonds denominated in an emerging market currency but are essentially default free. Regulation or differences in tax treatment occasionally have also played a role.

Beginning in 2001, the World Bank has allowed its *borrowers* to request a local-currency swap. That request is considered on a case-by-case basis, depending on whether current market conditions allow for a mutually advantageous outcome to be achieved. Following such a swap, the World Bank would face net liabilities in hard currency (as it normally does) while the emerging market that engaged in the swap would face net liabilities in its own currency. While there has been some interest in these local-currency swaps, no transactions have taken place to date, perhaps owing to initial learning barriers.

Recent proposals have sought to generalize this type of approach so as to fully exploit its benefits for emerging market countries. Levy-Yeyati (2003) argues that the role of the IFIs in issuing debt denominated in emerging market currencies could be expanded. He points out that a number of emerging market residents move their money abroad for a number of reasons, including a desire to decrease their vulnerability to possible government default. While those residents are unwilling to hold the credit risk of their own country, they may be willing to hold its currency risk because much of their consumption basket is in their local currency. The IFIs could issue risk-free local-currency debt, perhaps making it more attractive by indexing it to local inflation. The IFIs could then lend to the country without creating any currency mismatches in their balance sheets. The crowding-out effect on domestic credit markets may not be large, as some of those funds would have fled the country anyway.

Eichengreen, Hausmann, and Panizza (2002) suggest that the IFIs could issue in a basket of local-currency units indexed to the CPI of a number of emerging market countries. The pooling of currencies would help that market achieve a critical mass. The IFIs could simultaneously arrange a series of swaps with emerging market countries that had issued hard currency debt. However, if the swaps were arranged directly with emerging market country governments, the IFIs would face a default risk. If the swaps were arranged through an intermediary (which would then absorb, but also charge for, the default risk), the transactions costs could be large, partly because the swap markets between emerging market currencies and the world's major currencies are not very liquid. For a comprehensive critique of these proposals, see Goldstein and Turner (2004).

---

may result from external shocks or losses in investor confidence. Indeed, inflation-indexed debt exposes the borrower to less uncertainty than does foreign-currency debt (Box 1). Moreover, CPI-indexed debt provides as much policy discipline and investor protection as do short-term debt and foreign-currency debt.

A potential objection to issuing inflation-indexed debt is that it may lead to an economy-wide culture of sweeping CPI indexation, up to and including wage contracts. This would reduce real wage flexibility and weaken the effectiveness of stabilization policies. The example of Chile has often been mentioned in this context, but in that case a broader use of CPI indexation seems to have been specifically encouraged (Herrera and Valdés, 2003). In general, there is no automatic link between the currency of denomination of public and private liabilities and the denomination of other contracts in the economy. Another potential problem in some cases is the need for timely and reliable measurement of the CPI.

An alternative form of indexation that requires less statistical capacity is indexation to a market-determined domestic interest rate, that is, floating-rate debt. However, floating-rate debt implies higher debt repayments during bad times, whereas inflation-indexed debt is usually either acyclical or provides a slight hedge. From the perspective of decoupling government solvency from shifts in confidence and external shocks, floating-rate debt shares many of the disadvantages of foreign-currency debt.

Pension reforms and financial regulation often have important implications for the development of the domestic debt markets. A shift toward a fully funded pension system is often especially significant, because pension funds have a natural interest in debt securities carrying a relatively low default risk, and denominated in CPI units or local currency. Regulation that induces pension funds to invest a significant portion of assets locally may further enhance that interest. Of course, regulation that forces investors to hold long-term local-currency debt may also generate a temptation to reduce the debt burden through inflation or depreciation, and makes it easier for governments to overborrow. This temptation is somewhat mitigated by a large constituency of local-currency debt holders, who may pressure the government to follow sound fiscal and monetary policies. Moreover, if domestic banks hold large amounts of public debt, the government may be reluctant to provoke a crisis in which sovereign default would turn into a banking crisis. While the costs of financial repression will typically exceed its benefits, a greater share of long-term local-currency debt may be a welcome by-product.

While governments are seeking to establish credibility and develop domestic debt markets, they can undertake steps that help insulate the economy from external and confidence shocks, even in the presence of substantial shares of short-term debt or foreign-currency debt. Three such steps are mentioned briefly here. First, countries can avoid a bunching of repayment obligations, maintain adequate reserve levels, and manage reserves appropriately.[6] Second,

---

[6]International Monetary Fund and World Bank (2001); and IMF (2000a).

there is a trade-off between low debt levels and a less crisis-prone debt structure: with low debt levels, the public sector would remain solvent even after a depreciation; this reduces the urgency to move away from foreign-currency-denominated debt. Third, the importance of public sector vulnerabilities for the economy as a whole depends on conditions in other sectors, especially mismatches in the private financial sector and the flexibility of exports in responding to a depreciation.

Debt Issued on International Markets

Over the past two decades, some international financial institutions (IFIs) may have helped foster the creation of a market for internationally issued bonds in emerging market currencies. The IFIs have often been among the first parties to issue bonds denominated in emerging market currencies that had not previously been used in international bonds (Box 3, p. 21). The IFIs' main motivation for issuing bonds denominated in emerging market currencies, typically in combination with exchange rate swaps, has been to reduce their borrowing costs. At the same time, however, many residents of emerging markets may have borrowed internationally in their own currency as the counterparts in such swaps.

IV   Explicit Seniority in Privately Held Sovereign Debt

As described in Section II, the absence of explicit seniority is a striking difference between sovereign and corporate debt. This section argues that explicit seniority in sovereign debt—and, more generally, contractual innovations that help protect creditors from the consequences of future additional borrowing by the debtor country—could potentially play a useful role by promoting safer debt structures, discouraging overborrowing, and lowering interest costs for countries with moderate debt levels. However, this section is only a first pass at the issue, and a more thorough analysis of its consequences in different situations as well as its practical feasibility and impact on crisis resolution is warranted.[1]

Economic Role of Seniority

The traditional argument for the existence of senior debt is that it prevents debt dilution (Fama and Miller, 1972). Debt dilution is analogous to the dilution of equity through new equity issues. When new debt is issued, the recovery value of the debt has to be shared among more creditors in the event of insolvency; thus, dilution leads to a reduction in the repayment expected by each claim holder. New creditors are compensated for this effect through higher interest rates. But the initial creditors are not: for them, dilution means a capital loss. Anticipating this possibility, they may either require higher interest rates at the outset or refuse to lend altogether. Thus, the possibility of debt dilution may ultimately backfire on the debtor. But if the *original* creditors were senior—in other words, if creditors that lent earlier

had priority over those that lent later—they would be less concerned about subsequent debt issues, because in the event of bankruptcy they would be repaid first. Thus, first-in-time seniority may serve as an antidote to debt dilution.

At the corporate level, the case for senior debt is particularly strong when managers pursue their own agendas (Hart, 1995; Hart and Moore, 1995). Self-interested managers may have incentives to overborrow—for example, to finance projects that give them private benefits, to make the firm as large as possible, or to keep their jobs in a situation when it would in fact be efficient to liquidate the firm. If existing debt can be diluted, it is easy to overborrow, because new capital receives a share of the debt recovery value corresponding to its share in total debt outstanding. This is not the case when the new debt is junior: the presence of senior debt can thus serve as a disciplining device.

The dilution problem has become increasingly relevant to emerging market debt. For dilution to play a role, two conditions must be met. First, there must be a substantial chance of default or restructuring: as long as repayment remains safe, new debt issues are not a cause of concern for existing creditors. Second, debt must be issued to different groups of creditors over time. This would not be the case, for example, if emerging market governments kept borrowing from essentially the same group of banks, as happened during the 1970s and 1980s. However, in a case such as Argentina in the 1990s, which issued 156 bonds to a wide base of customers, dilution of earlier debt by later issues may have been intense. The same is true for other recent default or restructuring cases. For example, in the first half of 1998, Russia and Ukraine continued accessing capital markets through new debt issues at rapidly rising interest rates, thereby sharply diluting the existing debt stock.

One sign that the dilution problem is relevant in emerging market debt is that creditors seem to be making efforts to protect themselves against dilution. For example, one of the two Eurobonds that creditors were offered in Ecuador's 2000 debt exchange contained a "principal reinstatement" clause, which provided for an automatic upward adjustment in principal

---

Note: The author of this section is Jeromin Zettelmeyer.

[1]Gelpern (2004) argues that explicit seniority may result in a more predictable and less complicated debt restructuring process. Establishing a fixed priority ranking among creditors eliminates one aspect of the creditor collective action problem: the "race to the courthouse," whereby creditors seek an advantage by being the first to litigate. However, it can also be argued that an explicit seniority ranking would complicate debtor-creditor negotiations, because senior creditors have an incentive to agree quickly to a large haircut that leaves junior creditors with nothing (see Zettelmeyer, forthcoming, for a discussion).

in the event of a default. The face value of the bond-holder's claim was to increase by a given amount in the event that Ecuador defaulted on the new bonds after the restructuring (30 percent if a default occurred in the first three years after issuance, and gradually declining to zero after 10 years). Thus, incumbent bondholders received (temporary) protection from dilution that might result from new debt issuance.

The dilution problem could be eliminated if, in the event of a debt restructuring, creditor claims were served in the order in which the debt was issued. With this "first-in-time" seniority, initial creditors would be repaid (possibly in full), whereas the most recent creditors would receive much less, and possibly nothing.[2] If credible and enforceable, this could have desirable effects on the structure, cost, and amount of public borrowing. Explicit seniority could benefit the debt *structure* by reducing the incentive to issue debt forms that are hard to dilute, such as short-term foreign-currency debt. It could also lower the *costs* of borrowing at moderate levels of debt, because creditors would not have to worry about debt dilution in the future. Finally, by eliminating the possibility of issuing debt at the expense of previous creditors, seniority could reduce the incentives to *overborrow*. This said, countries with high levels of debt would find tighter market access and higher costs if they were to adopt a first-in-time seniority rule. This is an inherent drawback of any mechanism that reduces debt dilution and needs to be taken into consideration when evaluating the possible adoption of a seniority rule.

The following subsections elaborate on these points before turning to the question of how seniority-like features could in practice be introduced into sovereign debt. A number of obstacles and difficulties are discussed. While it is too early to say whether such difficulties could be resolved, the section suggests that consideration could be given to creating an international debt registry that would make it easier to monitor both total indebtedness and the contractual terms under which public debt is issued. This would be a necessary (albeit not sufficient) step for the development of an explicit seniority structure based on debt contracts, and may also have benefits of its own.

Effects of Seniority on the Quantity and Price of Debt

The benefits of making incumbent sovereign debt senior are most obvious when governments are bi-

ased toward excessive borrowing.[3] Diluting existing debt makes it easier for politicians to finance activities that may not be in the taxpayer's best interest. Examples include consumption or investment that benefit special interests, fiscal expansions ahead of elections, or—instead of politically costly reforms or restructurings—"gambles for redemption," whereby the dilution of existing debt may allow new government borrowing even when it is generally known that the country is insolvent. This may postpone a crisis, but the default, when it finally happens, will be much larger.

Seniority could also help curb overborrowing that arises even without a political bias toward excessive borrowing, purely as a consequence of the inability of the debtor to commit to not dilute the existing debt (Sachs and Cohen, 1982; Kletzer, 1984; Detragiache, 1994; and Eaton and Fernandez, 1997). Suppose that a country would like to borrow up to a given debt level. Once it has done so, it will generally have an incentive to borrow some more, because the dilution effect implies that new debt can be placed relatively cheaply. This will lead to excessive borrowing from the country's original perspective and—as it is anticipated by creditors—to higher interest rates. As a result, the country is worse off than if it had been able to commit to the original debt level. Seniority can rectify this problem by acting as a substitute for commitment: the debtor can credibly promise to the initial creditors that it will refrain from additional borrowing, because seniority eliminates the possibility of dilution.

Senior debt could also reduce borrowing costs for countries with low levels of debt; these countries might end up borrowing *more*. At present, the possibility of future debt dilution makes emerging market countries' debt relatively expensive even at moderate levels. As a result, governments that want to "play it safe" and keep their borrowing costs down have an incentive to borrow less than desirable, that is, below the level at which they would want to borrow if they could commit to not dilute (Bolton and Jeanne, 2004; and Zettelmeyer, forthcoming). With debt seniority acting as a binding promise to not dilute, countries with levels of debt that are low relative to sustainable levels would be able to borrow more, at equal or lower interest rates than would prevail in the absence of seniority.

As suggested above, any mechanism that limits debt dilution could impede debt dilution when it is in fact desirable. Consider a situation in which a (sol-

---

[2]In a variant of first-in-time seniority, time units could be calendar years, for example. All debt issued within a given year would have equal priority. Debt issued in year t would have absolute priority over debt issued in year $t-1$.

[3]The IMF's *World Economic Outlook* (September 2003, Chapter 3) suggests that overborrowing—defined as public debt that is higher than what can be repaid based on a country's fiscal track record—is widespread among developing countries and emerging market borrowers.

vent) country suffers an adverse shock that would require large additional financing. Issuing *junior* debt could be prohibitively expensive, because the probability of a debt crisis is now higher. In such a case, it might be in the interest of the incumbent creditors to allow dilution—in other words, allow new debt issues at the same, or even a higher, level of seniority as the existing debt—in order to provide the liquidity that might stave off a debt crisis. This is similar to the logic of "debtor in possession" financing mechanisms in corporate bankruptcy, whereby creditors may waive their seniority in order to allow the firm to access new money. A mechanism for waiving seniority in such situations could be useful. However, coordinating creditors on waiving seniority may be difficult in practice.

Collateralized debt shares some features with legally senior debt, but also suffers from some specific—and potentially serious—disadvantages. Like legally senior debt, fully collateralized debt cannot be diluted and may discourage overborrowing and lower the costs of responsible borrowing.[4] However, issuing collateralized debt is possible only for countries that have assets abroad or large cash flows originating in other jurisdictions. More important, promoting collateralized debt may be counterproductive if the basic problem is an inherent government bias to overborrow. With standard debt, the possibility of default would deter investors from lending to an irresponsible government. In contrast, collateralized debt could make it possible for lending to continue, effectively at the expense of future governments and generations.

Effects of Seniority on Debt Structure

Introducing seniority could have an impact not only on the quantity and price of debt but also on its structure. In the absence of explicit seniority, creditors may have an incentive to seek "de facto seniority" by opting for debt instruments that are hard to dilute, such as short-term debt (Sachs and Cohen, 1982; Kletzer, 1984; Chamon, 2002; Bolton and Jeanne, 2004). If maturities are short, lenders can refuse to roll over (or roll over at higher interest rates) as soon as they perceive an attempt to dilute. In contrast, if maturities are long, lenders are captive, and will suffer a capital loss.

Dilution fears could also create an incentive to borrow in debt forms that are relatively difficult to restructure, for example, through international bonds rather than domestic bonds or bank loans. If a coun-

try is able to repay some debt, but not all, it may default selectively on the instruments that can be renegotiated more easily. Once everyone has realized this, however, it will only be possible to issue hard-to-restructure instruments (Bolton and Jeanne, 2004; Lipworth and Nystedt, 2001).[5]

The implication of the bias toward short maturities is to make debt more crisis prone. The bias toward debt instruments that are relatively hard to restructure deepens crises when they occur and impedes restructurings that could have avoided major defaults. Seniority could help prevent costly crises by removing these biases.

Approaches and Obstacles in Implementing Explicit Seniority

An explicit, first-in-time seniority structure could arise through one of three mechanisms. First, new statutes at the international level, created by an international treaty or an amendment of the IMF's articles (IMF, 2002b; and Bolton and Skeel, 2003). Second, national legislation whereby debtor governments would commit to repay debt—in the event of default—in the order in which it was issued. For such commitment to be credible in the eyes of investors, changes to the law would have to be hard to make, and the domestic judiciary would need to be strong and independent. Third, contractual provisions protecting bondholders from dilution by future debt issues; such provisions would be enforced by the courts of the country where the debt was issued. The remainder of this section focuses mainly on the third approach, because it seems promising and raises complex issues that have not been analyzed before.

The contractual approach would loosely follow the example of creditor protections in corporate bond covenants. Specifically, the debt contract between an initial creditor and the debtor could contain a covenant prohibiting the debtor from issuing any subsequent debt unless future creditors agreed to be contractually subordinated to the initial creditor's claim. To enforce this covenant, senior creditors would need to be given the power to declare a default and accelerate if debtors fail to ensure that future creditors are subordinated. The next creditor's contract would then include a similar clause with respect to future debt, and so on. This sequence of contracts might generate a priority structure that gives senior creditors a legal

---

[4]On public sector collateralized borrowing, see IMF (2003d); and Chalk (2002).

[5]Debt restructurings in the 1990s seemed to reflect an implicit, though evolving, de facto seniority structure (Zettelmeyer, forthcoming).

Box 4. Enforcing Contractual Seniority

Establishing a feasible contractual priority structure based on time of issue requires solving two enforcement problems. First, assuming that outstanding claims define a consistent legal priority structure, this structure must be enforceable in the event of a restructuring. Second, a mechanism must be found that ensures that the priority structure is defined consistently. In particular, debtors have to be prevented from issuing new claims in contravention of earlier contracts, that is, claims that are not explicitly subordinated to those of previous creditors. The resolution of both these problems will most likely require the establishment of both debtor-creditor and intercreditor obligations.

Resolving the first problem—enforcing contractual priority in a default—requires giving senior creditors the legal basis to sue junior creditors who receive payments in contravention of their order of priority. To provide certainty, this legal basis is likely to require privity of contract between the senior creditor and the junior creditors. Specifically, the junior creditor would need to enter into a contract with the senior creditor that provides that the

junior creditor will not receive any payments from the debtor until the senior creditor is paid in full.

Making sure that the above framework is established also presents some challenges. Contrary to the case in which *existing* creditors agree to subordinate themselves to future creditors, as in the case of debtor-in-possession-type financing (Buchheit and Gulati, 2002), existing contracts must contain covenants that ensure that *future* creditors subordinate themselves in a way that gives senior creditors comfort that their priority can be enforced. The basic instrument for achieving this would be to give senior creditors the power to declare a default and accelerate if debtors fail to ensure that future creditors are subordinated to them. However, this is a fairly blunt instrument. Notably, if new creditors are not subordinated and previous creditors accelerate, they will not be able to enforce the seniority of their claims with respect to the most recent group of new creditors. This said, the threat of acceleration and technical default may conceivably provide sufficient discipline to the debtor for a consistent contractual priority structure to get off the ground.

basis to sue junior creditors in the event that seniority is violated in a default (Box 4).[6]

An explicit first-in-time seniority structure in sovereign debt could conceivably be undermined by debt issues that are formally subordinated but have shorter maturities and thus require earlier repayment. Indeed, to the extent that this is possible, first-in-time seniority might have perverse effects on the debt structure at high levels of debt, as it may lead sovereigns in distress to issue debt of even shorter maturities than under the present system. In the contractual approach, a possible solution could be an intercreditor provision to relinquish payments received 90 days prior to a formal default to the senior creditor. Alternatively, bond covenants could stipulate the suspension of payments to junior creditors—or their redirection to a trustee—prior to a formal default, upon observing prespecified signs of debt distress (e.g., when debt service capacity indicators cross certain thresholds). Finally, covenants could be added that effectively give senior creditors veto power over the issuance of short-term debt, by granting them the right to ask for early repayment.[7]

As is often the case with financial innovation, first-in-time seniority would add complexity to the debt instruments. Financial market participants would need to keep track of the seniority status of the various bonds when pricing them. Methods to price bonds with different degrees of seniority would have to be developed. It is possible that this additional complexity would make sovereign debt less attractive and raise borrowing costs, at least until markets became accustomed to the new system.

A further caveat is that highly indebted countries might not benefit from a switch to a first-in-time seniority regime. A new creditor would rank junior to all preexisting claims, and would hence need to be compensated by a higher interest rate, or could even refuse to lend at all if the risk of default were sufficiently high (Box 5). A similar problem might apply to countries that are liable to suffer from large adverse shocks that would increase their financing needs significantly. For many countries, however, this would be just a transitional problem. Under a *pari passu* regime, countries tend to overborrow because dilution lowers the costs of obtaining additional debt. Under a seniority regime, countries would have an incentive to maintain lower debt levels but, in some cases, they may need to reduce their debt levels before they are able to

---

[6]The IFIs (and possibly other official creditors) would be excluded from an explicit priority structure for privately held debt. This would not imply giving them legal seniority—rather, their seniority status would remain legally indeterminate with regard to the debt instruments whose seniority was governed by the new system. First-in-time seniority in privately held sovereign debt would thus have no bearing on the issue of IFI seniority.

[7]An analogous problem is that first-in-time seniority could be undermined through collateralized debt issues. Again, this prob-

lem would have to be dealt with by explicitly limiting or ruling out such issues through provisions in bond contracts.

Box 5. Effect on Borrowing Costs of a Switch to First-in-Time Seniority

As argued earlier, the main effect of first-in-time seniority on the quantity of countries' borrowing would be to reduce incentives to overborrow. After countries and markets have adjusted to the new regime, one would expect to see fewer countries at or close to unsustainable debt levels. In addition, borrowing costs would be lower, because spreads would no longer reflect the risk of future debt dilution.

However, the effect of a switch to first-in-time seniority *on impact*—for given outstanding debt stocks—might be to either raise or lower borrowing costs, depending on the size of countries' existing debt stocks. Countries with low debt levels would see their borrowing costs fall, whereas countries with high debt levels would see borrowing costs rise, and might even be cut off from additional net borrowing altogether. This is because at low debt levels, a creditor buying an extra unit of debt under first-in-time seniority would expect to be senior in the event of a default (because default would only occur after substantial accumulation of subsequent debt). In contrast, under the present regime this creditor would expect to rank equally, in the event of default, as the holders of debt issued subsequently. For very large outstanding debt levels, and a correspondingly high probability of a debt crisis in the near future, the opposite is true: a new creditor would expect to rank junior to most outstanding debt, and would consequently want to be compensated by higher interest rates than under the present system.

The argument is illustrated in the figure below. This assumes that the country in question has a *minimum* recovery value of debt, denoted $\underline{D}$, and a *maximum* sustainable debt level of $\bar{D}$. Under first-in-time seniority, an extra debt unit issued when actual debt is lower than $\underline{D}$ is risk free ($r^S(D) = \underline{r}$ for $D < \underline{D}$), as the new creditor will have first claim to the certain recovery value. In contrast, under the present system, even the very first debt unit issued is risky ($r^P(0) > \underline{r}$), because in the event

of default its holder would have to share the recovery value with the holders of all subsequently issued debt.

As D approaches $\bar{D}$, borrowing costs under seniority would go to infinity, because in the event of default, any new unit of debt would be junior to all other debt units and would receive nothing. In contrast, $r^P(\bar{D})$ is finite because new debt continues to enjoy a positive claim to the debt recovery value; as such, investors expect a positive return even when default is certain. Consequently, the *marginal* borrowing cost curves $r^S(D)$ and $r^P(D)$ must intersect at some debt level between $\underline{D}$ and $\bar{D}$. (The corresponding *average* borrowing cost curves—not depicted here—intersect at a higher D than shown in the figure below, because borrowing costs on the inframarginal units would be lower under seniority than under the present system.)

Marginal Borrowing Costs

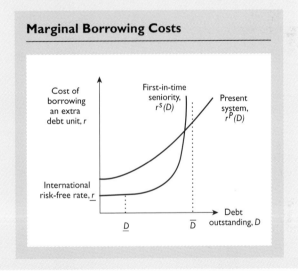

secure a reduction in their borrowing costs. These countries would have to gradually reduce their debt burdens to levels that are viewed as reasonably safe before issuing senior debt. Alternatively, they could incorporate seniority clauses that do not become effective immediately, but instead stipulate that the debt will become senior to new debt issued after a specified time interval (say, five years). This would allow time to adjust from high debt levels, and provide a commitment to doing so.

Before concluding, it is worth emphasizing that there may be alternative contractual ways of reducing the dilution problem while not establishing a full-fledged legal priority structure in the event of default. One possibility would be to give creditors contractual options that provide them with some control over the debtors' subsequent borrowing be-

havior or allow them to renegotiate in the event of new borrowing. At the most basic level, contracts could include put options allowing debtors to ask for early repayment in the event that certain limits on total debt are exceeded. Alternatively, future debt issues could trigger changes in the payment terms of existing bonds in a way that offsets the loss of value inflicted upon their holders by the new borrowing. These alternative approaches may go a considerable way toward addressing the dilution problem without raising the legal difficulties of full-fledged first-in-time seniority. Because they do not have the effect of making the outstanding debt stock legally senior relative to future debt issues, they might also avoid possible transitional problems associated with full-fledged first-in-time seniority.

Conclusions

Explicit seniority in privately held sovereign debt, or other possible enhancements in debt contracts that significantly reduce the scope for debt dilution, could have benefits in terms of discouraging overborrowing, lowering the debt costs of responsible borrowers, and reducing the incentives to adopt risky debt structures. These benefits would need to be balanced against a potential cost, namely, the possibility that countries with high levels of debt would find it more difficult to access international capital markets than they do under the present system. Countries with more moderate debt levels—but which nevertheless pay a substantial risk premium—could thus stand to gain the most from adopting a seniority regime. Other countries might need to find ways to reduce their debt to safer levels before the benefits could be secured.

This said, the analysis of both the feasibility and overall effects of seniority-like features in sovereign debt would need to be extended before reaching a more definitive judgment on the issue. In particular, further analysis would be needed in three areas: (1) the impact of seniority on crisis resolution (an aspect not addressed in this paper); (2) the legal and operational feasibility of a contractual seniority structure; and (3) the desirability and feasibility of enhancements in bond contracts that might protect bondholders from dilution without the need to create a legal seniority structure.

One possible step that would not seem to depend on how the verdict on the usefulness and practicality of explicit seniority ultimately turns out is the creation of an international official debt registry publishing the terms of all public debt contracts.[8] While such a registry might be a necessary step toward a contractual seniority structure, it could also be of value more generally. Greater transparency in the level and structure of sovereign debt might contribute to the efficiency of the debt market, and would play a helpful role in the context of debt restructuring operations. Although the costs of establishing a debt registry should be evaluated carefully, the public good aspect of information is an argument for officially sponsoring such a registry.

---

[8]Such a registry has been proposed on several occasions in the past—for example, by Allen (1988); Kaeser (1990); and Eaton (2002).

V Expanding the Set of Instruments: Indexation to Real Variables

Most proposals for reform of the international financial architecture have taken the set of available financial instruments as given. This section asks whether greater use of underutilized instruments could be beneficial in providing countries with insurance and reducing the likelihood of crises. Debt sustainability hinges on developments in real variables, such as exports and GDP. Adverse shocks to these variables often prompt debt crises.[1] For some countries, such shocks routinely take the form of adverse developments in commodity prices, natural disasters, or declines in imports by trading partners. For others, changes in economic growth are more difficult to relate to specific events or sectors of the economy.

Debt indexed to real variables has been proposed as a way of mitigating changes in debt sustainability that might result from real shocks (Box 6). This section explores the role of debt (or insurance) contracts indexed to real variables, which include

- variables that are largely outside the control of the country's authorities and in many cases can be measured in a relatively straightforward manner—such as commodity prices, natural disasters, or imports by a country's main trading partners; and

- broader measures of economic activity that are partly within the control of the country's authorities and are typically measured by the country's own statistical agencies—such as the country's own exports or GDP.

The relative merits of indexing to variables in these two groups will depend on individual country

characteristics such as the sources of shocks, the reliability of the statistical information, and the perceived credibility of the authorities. In fact, while indexation to broader measures such as GDP would likely provide greater insurance benefits, potential investors might be concerned about the authorities' incentives to tamper with GDP data or even undertake less-growth-oriented policies, as suggested by some studies (e.g., Krugman, 1988). As indexation to variables outside the control of the authorities has been extensively treated in many previous studies, this section provides more detailed information about indexation to variables partly within the control of the authorities, whose properties and challenges are relatively underexplored.

Benefits of Indexation to Real Variables

Indexing bond repayments to real variables such as GDP or exports, or some of their key determinants (such as natural disasters, commodity prices, or trading partners' total output or imports), would tend to promote debt sustainability (or raise the level of sustainable debt) by stabilizing variables such as the debt-to-GDP ratio—thereby providing a number of benefits to borrowing countries:

- If the economy falls onto a path of persistent weak growth, the smaller increases in the debt-to-GDP ratio resulting from indexation would reduce the likelihood of default and debt crises.

- Governments would find it easier to maintain a smooth path for tax rates and essential public services despite fluctuations in economic growth. The need to pay higher interest rates in years of rapid growth might even make it more difficult for governments to boost noninterest spending unsustainably during times of economic boom.

- By acting as an "automatic-stabilizer," real indexation would reduce pressures on governments to engage in procyclical fiscal policy. Emerging markets are often forced to tighten

---

Note: The authors of this section are Eduardo Borensztein and Paolo Mauro.

[1]Slow growth underlies many debt crises, including the Latin American debt crisis of the 1980s and the debt crisis of the highly indebted poor countries (HIPCs) in the 1980s and 1990s. The growth slowdown that began in Argentina in 1998 contributed to its recent debt crisis—though vulnerabilities had built up previously (IMF, 2003f). Several studies find that slow economic growth or high debt help predict debt crises (Detragiache and Spilimbergo, 2001; Easterly, 2001; Kraay and Nehru, 2003; and Manasse, Roubini, and Schimmelpfennig, 2003).

Box 6. Proposals for Indexation to Real Variables

A first wave of interest in indexing debt to GDP, exports, or key commodity prices emerged in the aftermath of the debt crisis of the 1980s. Bailey (1983) suggested the conversion of debt into proportional claims on exports. Lessard and Williamson (1985) made the case for real indexation of debt claims. Krugman (1988) and Froot, Scharfstein, and Stein (1989) considered the relative merits of indexing debt to variables out of the debtor country's control (such as commodity prices) versus variables partially under the country's control (exports or GDP). At the time, a majority view within the academic community seemed, on balance, to emphasize the moral hazard costs rather than the insurance benefits of indexing to exports or GDP. The decline in commodity prices was fresh in people's minds as one of the causes of the debt crisis and—with commodities still representing a significant share of production and exports for some of the countries most affected—indexing to commodity prices seemed like a better idea.

A second wave of interest originated from Shiller's (1993, 2003) proposal to create "macro markets" for GDP-linked securities. In Shiller's proposal, these were to be perpetual claims on a fraction of a country's GDP. Barro (1995) shows that bonds ought to be indexed to consumption and government expenditure in a model of optimal debt management where the government seeks to smooth tax rates over time. But he suggests GDP-indexed bonds as a more realistic alternative with fewer problems related to moral hazard and measurement. This section analyzes a possibility related to Shiller's proposal: a bond whose coupon payments are indexed to GDP growth is equivalent to a plain vanilla bond combined with a security whose payoff depends on deviations of the issuing country's growth rate from a baseline. While Shiller security markets would have

to be set up from scratch, the possibility analyzed in this section might be easier to implement: it would require introducing an indexation clause in otherwise standard sovereign bonds.

For emerging market economies, the case for contingent debt contracts has received new impetus after the financial and debt crises of the 1990s. Caballero (2003) recommends that countries issue bonds with contingencies to commodity prices and other external variables of relevance to them (e.g., Chile should issue bonds indexed to the price of copper). Haldane (1999) argues that emerging markets would benefit from indexing debt to commodity prices. Daniel (2001) argues that many governments would benefit from hedging oil price risk through existing financial instruments and markets, and that international institutions should encourage them to explore this possibility. Drèze (2000a) suggests the use of GDP-indexed bonds as part of a strategy to restructure the debt of the poorest countries. Varsavsky and Braun (2002) make the case for restructuring Argentina's debt into GDP-indexed bonds.

Related proposals have also been made for advanced countries. Some investment banks in Sweden proposed to introduce GDP-indexed bonds in the mid-1990s. The idea received some support in official circles, but fell by the wayside partly because the National Debt Office at the time was focused on promoting greater use of inflation-indexed bonds (Englund, Becker, and Paalzow, 1997). Obstfeld and Peri (1998) suggest that individual governments in the European Union should issue perpetual euro-denominated liabilities indexed to domestic nominal per capita GDP growth. They argue that nominal rather than real indexing would protect securities holders against inflation. Drèze (2000b) makes a similar proposal for the EMU countries.

---

fiscal policies during economic downturns in an attempt to maintain credibility and access to international financial markets, as suggested by the sudden stops literature (Calvo, 2003).[2] But real indexation may be helpful more generally to governments that are seeking to stabilize the debt-to-GDP ratio, whether because of legal or constitutional constraints, agreements such as the Stability and Growth Pact, or inability to borrow beyond a certain level.

This section focuses on the insurance benefits of real indexation for the borrowing countries and their citizens. Yet, real indexation can be viewed more generally as a desirable vehicle for international risk-sharing and as a way of avoiding the disruptions arising from formal default. It thus has a number of potential benefits for international investors:

- International investors would also benefit from a lower frequency of formal default, which often results in costly litigation/renegotiation and is thus disruptive even to large private financial institutions that might be considered risk neutral.

- Citizens of lending countries would appreciate the ability to invest in assets whose return is linked to other countries' fortunes. As countries' incomes are far from being perfectly correlated, this would provide a welcome diversification opportunity.

---

[2]Gavin and Perotti (1997) find that during deep recessions the fiscal surplus typically *increases* in Latin American countries, whereas it *falls* in OECD countries. They also find that public spending is far more procyclical in Latin American countries than it is in OECD countries—a result confirmed by Talvi and Végh (2000) and the *World Economic Outlook* (September 2003, Chapter 3) for emerging markets and developing countries more generally.

• Finally, for the case of GDP indexation, financial market participants might be interested in the opportunity to take a position on countries' future growth prospects. This is already possible to some extent through countries' stock markets, but these are often not representative of the economy as a whole, especially in emerging market countries.

Real Variables Beyond the Control of the Country's Authorities

Some shocks that have a major economic impact are largely beyond the control of the country's authorities. For the vast majority of countries, fluctuations in world commodity prices are essentially given. Of course, countries may wish to diversify their production, export, and revenue structures, but this takes time and may not always be desirable. Similarly, there is little countries can do to avoid natural disasters, though investments in preparedness and relocation of activities to less disaster-prone areas help mitigate the consequences of disasters. Finally, except for a few very large economies, countries typically must take as given the economic performance of their trading partners.

Bonds whose repayments are linked to such variables are worth considering. Bonds whose repayments are indexed to commodity prices have been used, although rarely, since the 1800s. Insurance against natural disasters (including through catastrophe bonds—whose repayment is waived in the event of a catastrophe) is a much more recent innovation that is already widespread in the private sector, but has only been used by a handful of sovereigns. Bonds whose repayment is linked to trading partners' performance have not been previously used (or advocated), but their use would seem to be desirable.

Commodity Price Shocks

Shocks to commodity prices have important effects on debt sustainability for several countries where commodities are a sizable share of exports and GDP, and export taxes are a substantial share of total revenues. Shocks to prices of key imports, notably oil, are perhaps even more important for many developing countries, though insuring against these shocks has received less attention than shocks to exports. A number of studies suggest that changes in commodity prices (or, more generally, terms-of-trade shocks) can have a large impact on revenues and economic growth, though the exact

magnitude of the estimated impact differs considerably across studies.[3]

Most advanced countries have well-diversified production and export structures. The percentage share of the top export in total exports of goods amounts to more than one-third only for Iceland (fish) and Norway (oil) (Table 4).[4] Even for advanced countries for which commodities are often considered significant, such as Australia, the share of the top three exports in total exports is no more than a quarter.

For several developing countries and a few emerging markets, a single product or a few products constitute an overwhelming portion of total exports. Of the 27 emerging market countries for which data are available, 6 have more than 25 percent of exports in one commodity: Chile (copper, 27 percent), Colombia (oil, 29 percent), Egypt (oil, 27 percent), Kenya (tea, 28 percent), Venezuela (oil, 80 percent), and Zimbabwe (tobacco, 34 percent). However, of the emerging market countries with the largest bond market capitalization (Argentina, Brazil, Korea, Mexico, and Russia—on the basis of the EMBIG weights for 2000–03), only Russia's share of the top three exports is above one quarter.

As might be expected, the importance of commodity price shocks for economic performance differs considerably across countries. Collier and Dehn (2001) report that large adverse shocks to commodity prices are significantly associated with a decline in output growth for commodity-producing countries, though not for other countries. For the typical commodity producer, the worst shocks—in the lowest 2.5 percent of the shock distribution—are associated with a 7 percent output decline in the year of the shock and a cumulative 14 percent decline in the year of the shock and the following three years.[5] Shocks to commodity prices have widely different effects on tax revenues depending on the country under consideration. For example, changes in oil prices of reasonable magnitudes affect the revenues of oil-producing countries by several percentage points of GDP (IMF, 2000b).

---

[3]Using a broad panel of countries, Easterly and others (1993) find that a favorable terms-of-trade shock of 1 percentage point per annum was associated with an increase in the annual growth rate of real GDP per capita by 0.42 percentage points in the 1970s and 0.85 percentage points in the 1980s. Studies based upon vector autoregressions find that, for the typical emerging market country, only a small share of output fluctuations can be attributed to terms-of-trade shocks (Hoffmaister and Roldós, 1997).

[4]The data refer to 1999 and are drawn from UNCTAD (2001). Products are defined at the Standard Investment Trade Classification (SITC-3) level.

[5]Panel regressions estimated by IMF staff, though not reported in this paper for the sake of brevity, yield smaller and less significant coefficients for both commodity-producing and other countries.

Table 4. Percentage Share of the Top Three Exports in Total Exports, 1990–99

Country	Product 1	Export Share	Product 2	Export Share	Product 3	Export Share	Total Share of Top 3 Products
Advanced economies							
Iceland	Fresh fish	19.6	Aluminum	10.9	Preserved and smoked fish	7.4	37.8
Norway	Petroleum and crude oils	36.3	Gas	15.6	Fresh fish	15.0	66.8
Singapore	Thermionic cells	37.6	Data processing equipment	8.1	Parts and accessories	5.9	51.6
Finland	Paper and paperboard	20.1	Telecom equipment	17.3	Wood and wood products	8.8	46.2
Hong Kong SAR	Outer, knitted garments	19.7	Outer, women's garments	17.1	Thermionic cells	3.7	40.5
Ireland	Data processing equipment	14.9	Parts and accessories	11.7	Thermionic cells	9.2	35.7
Sweden	Telecom equipment	13.5	Paper and paperboard	9.0	Nitrogen compounds	8.8	31.3
Cyprus	Pharmaceutical products	14.6	Vegetables	8.0	Special transactions, others	6.2	28.8
New Zealand	Meat and edible meat offals	11.8	Milk and cream	8.5	Fruit and nuts	7.3	27.6
Canada	Passenger vehicles	12.7	Special transactions, others	7.8	Fruit and nuts	4.6	25.0
		14.5		6.0	Parts and accessories	4.3	24.8
Emerging market countries							
Venezuela	Petroleum and crude oils	35.3	Aluminum	9.9	Various forms of iron	7.0	52.2
Philippines	Special transactions, others	80.8	Thermionic cells	3.3	Data processing equipment	1.2	85.2
Colombia	Petroleum and crude oils	51.2	Coffee	11.4	Coal, lignite and peat	9.0	71.6
Kenya	Tea	28.8	Coffee	12.3	Refined petroleum products	7.2	48.3
Jordan	Fertilizers, crude	28.4	Fertilizers, manufactured	10.4	Pharmaceutical products	8.2	47.0
Chile	Copper	25.6	Ores, metal concentrates	10.6	Fruit and nuts	10.3	46.5
Zimbabwe	Unmanufactured tobacco	27.2	Various forms of iron	12.1	Cotton	7.1	46.5
Israel	Pearls, precious stones	33.4	Telecom equipment	6.8	Data processing equipment	5.8	46.0
Peru	Gold, nonmonetary	30.1	Copper	11.1	Ores, metal concentrates	4.2	45.5
Egypt	Refined petroleum products	20.1	Petroleum and crude oils	12.2	Cotton	10.3	42.7
		27.4		8.4		6.8	42.6
Developing economies							
Algeria	Gas	50.9	Petroleum and crude oils	16.9	Refined petroleum products	10.0	77.9
Faroe Islands	Fresh fish	41.7	Preserved and smoked fish	39.7	Crustaceans and mollusks	15.0	96.5
St. Lucia	Fruit and nuts	65.9	Alcoholic beverages	14.9	Outer, knitted garments	5.5	86.4
Oman	Petroleum and crude oils	63.6	Passenger vehicles	12.7	Refined petroleum products	5.8	82.2
Syrian Arab Republic	Petroleum and crude oils	74.4	Vegetables	3.9	Fruit and nuts	2.6	80.8
Grenada	Spices	64.3	Meal, wheat or meslin flour	5.9	Fresh fish	4.5	74.6
St. Vincent and the Grenadines	Fruit and nuts	53.1	Meal, wheat or meslin flour	10.8	Rice	10.2	74.0
Togo	Cotton	47.8	Fertilizers, crude	15.0	Construction material	11.2	74.0
Belize	Sugar	33.5	Preserved fruits	26.5	Crustaceans and mollusks	11.6	71.7
Macau	Outer, knitted garments	25.9	Outer, women's garments	23.8	Undergarments	20.0	69.6
		38.8		16.2		13.7	68.7

Source: UNCTAD (2001).

Note: Within each group, countries are ranked by the total share of the top three exports. Ten countries with the highest export shares are reported. The country group averages refer to the whole sample.

Both the IMF and the World Bank have long provided facilities specifically designed to help countries adjust to large terms-of-trade shocks. The IMF has used a number of facilities including the Compensatory Financing Facility (CFF), established in the 1960s to assist countries experiencing either a sudden shortfall in export earnings or an increase in cereal import costs caused by fluctuating world commodity prices. Yet, limits to administrative capacity imply that only a few large terms-of-trade shocks will lead to loans in the context of programs supported by the IFIs. More important, with shocks to commodity prices being highly persistent (Cashin, Liang, and McDermott, 2000), these loans facilitate adjustment to adverse shocks and the resulting lower income levels, but they are not designed to provide insurance or maintain income levels through state-contingent transfers.

Countries seem to be reluctant to insure themselves against commodity risks through financial instruments. Until the 1980s, government and multilateral interventions aimed at price stabilization in commodity markets were commonplace. A consensus among academics and policymakers seems to have emerged since then for a shift away from market intervention and toward management of commodity risks through financial instruments (see, e.g., Claessens and Duncan, 1993; Dehn, Gilbert, and Varángis, forthcoming).[6] In the context of that shift, researchers in academia and international institutions, notably the World Bank, spurred a debate on the merits of commodity-price-linked bonds. Such bonds could be viewed as a way for countries to hedge against changes in commodity prices even in cases where futures or forwards of a sufficiently long maturity are either absent or too costly. Nevertheless, commodity-price-linked bonds have been used only in a limited number of instances.

Recent efforts to provide sovereigns with market-based insurance against commodity fluctuations do not appear to be attracting much interest. Since September 1999, the World Bank has offered risk management products linked to IBRD loan exposures, including swaps that seek to hedge against fluctuations in interest rates, currencies, and commodity prices. However, swaps that hedge against commodity price fluctuations have not been used by World Bank clients to date. Nor do sovereigns make much use of hedging opportunities even where active and liquid markets exist for futures and forwards on commodities with maturities extending beyond a few years, as is the case for oil (Daniel, 2001).

Sovereigns' reluctance to use financial instruments to hedge against commodity price fluctuations is not fully understood, though it may be related to the following factors:

- Insurance—even if incomplete—is already provided, to some extent, by the IFIs.

- Prices obtained by some countries for the particular quality of the commodities they produce may not be closely correlated with those observed on international exchanges.

- Regarding commodity-price-linked bonds more specifically, international investors often express a preference for separating exposure to country risks (through standard bonds) from exposure to commodity price risks (through existing markets for commodity price forwards and futures).

- Without hedging, the borrowing country does not need to share its gains on the upside; and it may force its lenders (through default) to share the downside.

- It may be politically difficult to pay for hedging, especially in the event that—with hindsight—this turns out to have been the wrong decision. This factor is not unique to sovereigns and may be one of the reasons why hedging remains more limited than might be expected even in the corporate world.[7]

Countries wishing to reduce volatility resulting from commodity price shocks could of course consider taking steps to diversify their economies. However, this process may take many years and some countries may even judge that their comparative advantage really lies in a few products. Hedging against commodity price fluctuations through financial instruments, including commodity-price-linked bonds, would therefore seem desirable for several countries.

Natural Disasters

Natural disasters take a massive human and economic toll on virtually all countries. Their impact relative to the size of the economy tends to be higher, the lower the degree of economic development and the smaller the size of the country under consideration. This is confirmed by considering the top five most devastating disasters, ranked by the direct loss of capital stock in percent of GDP, for vari-

---

[6]Shocks to commodity prices tend to be highly persistent, implying that schemes to stabilize commodity export earnings would be exceedingly costly (Cashin and others, 2000). Davis and others (2001) suggest that the record of stabilization funds for renewable resources is mixed.

[7]What would the president of an oil company say—after a rise in oil prices—to the treasurer who had hedged against the price change in the futures market? See Hull (2002, p. 74).

Table 5. Top Five Natural Disasters by Percent of GDP Lost

Country	Year	Direct Economic Loss (In percent of GDP)	Type of Disaster	Measure	Change in GDP Growth Rate (In percent)
Advanced economies					
Italy	1980	4.5	Earthquake	7.2 Richter	−2.6
Australia	1982	3.3	Drought	...	−5.7
Greece	1978	2.6	Earthquake	...	4.5
Japan	1995	2.5	Earthquake	7.2 Richter	0.5
Spain	1983	2.4	Flood	...	0.6
Emerging market countries					
Zimbabwe	1982	29.3	Drought	...	−9.7
El Salvador	1986	27.3	Earthquake	7.5 Richter	−1.2
Dominican Republic	1998	13.8	Hurricane	210 kph	−0.8
El Salvador	2001	10.9	Earthquake	6.1 Richter	−0.3
Chile	1985	9.1	Earthquake	...	−0.9
Developing countries (excluding small countries)					
Honduras	1998	38.0	Hurricane	270 kph	−2.0
Belize	2000	34.4	Hurricane	215 kph	6.7
Jamaica	1988	28.2	Hurricane	...	4.3
Nepal	1987	24.6	Flood	...	−2.8
Guatemala	1976	22.9	Earthquake	7.5 Richter	5.4
Small countries					
St. Lucia	1988	365.0	Hurricane	...	10.0
Mongolia	1996	171.6	Forest fire	80,000 km^2	−3.7
Vanuatu	1985	146.3	Cyclone	...	−4.6
Samoa	1991	138.9	Cyclone	167 kph	2.1
Dominica	1979	100.8	Hurricane	...	−30.1

Source: Emergency database (EM-DAT), compiled by Office of Foreign Disaster Assistance (OFDA) and Centre for Research on Epidemiology of Disasters (CRED).

Note: The definition of advanced countries follows that of the IMF's *World Economic Outlook*. The set of emerging market countries is the union of those defined as such by the International Finance Corporation, *Global Stock Market Factbook 2002*, and the JPMorgan Emerging Market Bond Index Global. Small countries are defined as those with GDP below $5 billion in 2002. The remaining countries are included in the set of developing countries. Direct economic loss is calculated using CRED's measure of direct damage to physical infrastructure as a result of the natural disaster.

ous groups of countries: advanced, emerging market, developing, and small (Table 5).[8] For advanced countries, the direct loss of capital stock attributable to specific natural disasters usually does not exceed a few percentage points of GDP. For emerging markets, this direct impact can occasionally be equivalent to more than 10 percentage points of GDP. For small developing countries, especially small islands, the impact can occasionally be equivalent to more

than a year's worth of output. The impact on the fiscal deficit and the trade deficit can also be equivalent to several percentage points of GDP (Freeman, Keen, and Mani, 2003). In many instances, the impact on the GDP growth rate is not commensurate with the direct loss in the capital stock, suggesting that indexation to GDP in these cases would not provide sufficient insurance.

A few countries are routinely affected by the same type of natural disaster: a few small islands are repeatedly hit by cyclones; other countries are particularly prone to earthquakes, or floods (Table 6). However, perhaps a majority of countries that are prone to natural disasters are affected by a variety of disasters, rather than a single type of event. This makes it even more difficult in these countries to estimate the likelihood of disasters and to obtain insurance contracts (or bond indexation clauses) than in countries where disasters always tend to be of the same type.

---

[8]Data are only available for the direct loss of capital in a sampled area affected by the disaster, and such estimates could be biased, particularly if they are made very soon after a disaster strikes. The overall effect on the economy is harder to gauge. The impact on income is likely greater in the immediate aftermath of the disaster, as demand by economic agents affected by the disaster declines and economic activity is disrupted more generally. Later on, however, growth may accelerate somewhat, as the economy rebuilds its capital stock and catches up toward its previous levels of activity.

Most natural disasters have a temporary impact on the fiscal deficit and the economy's growth rate. In the aftermath of a disaster, spending jumps to alleviate humanitarian emergencies and to begin reconstructing infrastructure. As far as the real economy is concerned, for most large disasters considered in Table 4, growth in the year of the disaster declined by a few percentage points but soon returned to its long-run trend, typically within one or two years following the disaster. Caselli and Malhotra (2004) find that, in most instances, natural disasters have no permanent impact on a country's long-run growth path, though they have a permanent effect on the level of income. From the narrow perspective of debt sustainability, most natural disasters may be viewed as creating repayment difficulties in the aftermath of the disaster, but not as affecting the country's ability or willingness to meet its external obligations on a permanent basis.

This set of facts has implications for whether countries are likely to be interested in insuring themselves against natural disasters, and for the types of insurance contracts that can be more efficient. Larger, more advanced economies are typically able to cope with natural disasters on their own, by letting the debt-to-GDP ratio rise in the aftermath of the disaster and gradually reducing it over a number of years, through slightly higher taxes or lower spending on other items. For emerging market countries, and especially developing countries, it is often difficult to muster sufficient funds from the private capital markets to cope with disasters. In many instances, the international community has therefore appropriately stepped in with aid and new lending. For its part, the IMF provides emergency assistance to countries that have experienced a natural disaster or are emerging from conflict.[9] At the same time, some natural disasters, even if seriously damaging, fail to capture international attention. And even when aid is provided by the international community, it is insufficient to prevent declines in income levels, and lending merely helps smooth the adjustment to a lower income level. Thus, disaster-prone countries might be expected to have a strong interest in obtaining insurance from the private sector. Both the World Bank and the Inter-American Development Bank have advocated greater use of insurance against natural disasters for some countries, and have sought to help country clients obtain such insurance from the markets (Gilbert and Kreimer, 1999; Inter-American Development Bank, 2002).

Despite the existence of markets for insurance against natural disasters, at present only a handful of countries use them. Insurance is available both directly from insurance companies and through innovative financial instruments such as catastrophe bonds, which waive some or all of the principal and interest repayments in the event of a prespecified catastrophe, or weather derivatives, which provide payouts in the event of temperatures or rainfall above or below prespecified trigger levels over a certain period. Sovereigns rarely opt for disaster insurance, even for their own property (Freeman, Keen, and Mani, 2003). Sovereigns rarely issue catastrophe bonds, though it is somewhat more common for private companies to do so.

The possible reasons for why countries do not often insure themselves against natural disasters include the following:

- In the case of small and poor countries, insurance companies may consider the size of the potential market too limited for them to incur the cost of estimating the likelihood of disasters.

- Insurance premiums may be high because of potential moral hazard: contracts normally provide for payoffs based upon actual losses rather than the intensity of the natural phenomenon, which could be measured, say, by the number of points on the Richter scale in the case of earthquakes. This tends to reduce countries' incentives to invest in preventive measures aimed at reducing the physical destruction that would result from disasters.

- Countries may expect the international community to step in with generous aid and financial support in response to disasters.

The international community could help countries meet a number of prerequisites to obtain insurance contracts against natural disasters from the private sector at a reasonable premium. These include historical data on previous events; appropriate infrastructure, such as weather stations, necessary for contracts based on specific measurements, such as rainfall or temperatures; and historical correlations of actual losses with the scale of events. Technical assistance in these areas, especially to small countries, might also be helpful.

Countries that are prone to natural disasters could be encouraged to consider insurance through the private markets. To mitigate possible disincentives, the international community could emphasize its readiness to step in with help even for countries that have obtained insurance from the private sector. One possibility might be for the international community to commit to providing emergency assistance, perhaps on a concessional basis, to countries deemed to have undertaken appropriate measures to mitigate the impact of possible disasters (Freeman, Keen, and Mani, 2003).

---

[9]Emergency loans are subject to the basic rate of charge and must be repaid within 3¼–5 years (without expectation of early repayment).

Table 6. Small Countries: Types of Disasters, 1975–2002

Country	Cumulative Damage (Millions of 2002 U.S. dollars)	GDP 2002 (Millions of U.S. dollars)	Cumulative Damage (Percent of GDP)	Number of Disasters	Most Frequent Types of Disasters
Afghanistan	601.6	...	...	56	21 floods, 19 earthquakes, 6 slides, 3 droughts, 4 cold waves
Albania	35.8	4,820	0.7	12	5 floods, 3 earthquakes, 1 cold wave, 1 avalanche
Antigua and Barbuda	106.9	720	14.8	7	6 hurricanes, 1 drought
Armenia	148.5	2,360	6.3	4	2 floods, 1 earthquake, 1 drought
Barbados	145.5	2,440	6.0	5	4 hurricanes, 1 flood
Belize	345.5	840	41.1	9	4 hurricanes, 3 floods, 1 cold wave, 1 tropical storm
Benin	11.9	2,700	0.4	17	10 floods, 4 droughts, 2 wildfires, 1 windstorm
Bhutan	3.7	570	0.6	4	2 floods, 1 cyclone, 1 wildfire
Bosnia and Herzegovina	163.6	...	...	4	1 windstorm, 1 slide, 1 flood, 1 drought
Burkina Faso	...	3,140	...	17	9 droughts, 6 floods, 2 insect infestations
Burundi	...	630	...	8	4 floods, 3 droughts, 1 windstorm
Cambodia	160.6	3,660	4.4	13	8 floods, 3 droughts, 2 famines
Cape Verde Islands	5.0	620	0.8	10	6 droughts, 1 tropical storm, 1 cyclone, 1 volcano, 1 famine
Central African Republic	0.2	1,060	0.0	11	5 floods, 2 windstorms, 2 wildfires, 2 droughts
Chad	112.8	1,970	5.7	26	13 droughts, 7 floods, 4 insect infestations, 2 windstorms
Comoros	65.1	250	26.0	7	4 cyclones, 2 volcanoes, 1 drought
Congo	0.1	3,010	0.0	5	4 floods, 1 drought
Djibouti	10.0	590	1.7	14	7 droughts, 6 floods, 1 windstorm
Dominica	128.1	250	51.2	7	7 hurricanes
Eritrea	6.1	...	...	5	3 droughts, 1 windstorm, 1 insect infestation
Fiji	813.6	1,830	44.5	25	17 cyclones, 3 floods, 2 droughts, 2 earthquakes, 1 windstorm
Gabon	...	4,960	...	1	1 flood
Gambia, The	...	350	...	15	9 droughts, 3 insect infestations, 3 floods
Georgia	2,425.0	3,450	70.3	9	4 earthquakes, 2 floods, 2 droughts, 1 windstorm
Grenada	29.1	410	7.1	4	2 hurricanes, 1 tropical storm, 1 flood
Guinea	12.9	3,210	0.4	8	3 floods, 3 droughts, 1 tornado, 1 earthquake
Guinea Bissau	...	200	0.0	12	6 floods, 3 insect infestations, 1 windstorm, 1 wildfire, 1 cyclone
Guyana	31.1	710	4.4	5	2 droughts, 2 floods, 1 slide
Haiti	289.3	3,550	8.1	32	19 floods, 5 hurricanes, 4 droughts, 2 windstorms
Kiribati	...	50	...	1	1 drought
Kyrgyzstan	239.1	1,600	14.9	8	3 slides, 3 earthquakes, 1 cold wave, 1 flood
Lao P.D.R.	387.6	1,860	20.8	23	12 floods, 7 droughts, 2 typhoons, 2 windstorms
Lesotho	...	800	...	14	5 windstorms, 5 droughts, 1 famine, 3 floods
Liberia	60.1	560	10.7	5	1 windstorm, 1 slide, 1 cold wave, 1 flood, 1 drought
Macedonia, Former Yugoslav Republic of	408.8	3,730	11.0	5	2 floods, 1 wildfire, 1 cold wave, 1 famine

Madagascar	2,495.5	4,560	54.7	31	22 cyclones, 6 droughts, 2 floods, 1 insect infestation
Malawi	37.3	1,930	1.9	23	14 floods, 6 droughts, 2 famines, 1 earthquake
Mauritania	54.0	990	5.5	25	12 droughts, 8 floods, 3 insect infestations, 1 windstorm, 1 tornado
Mauritius	1,445.8	4,560	31.7	15	14 cyclones, 1 drought
Micronesia, Federated States of	11.8	…	…	4	2 tropical storms, 1 typhoon, 1 drought
Moldova	195.8	1,630	12.0	7	4 floods, 2 windstorms, 1 drought
Mongolia	2,953.5	1,090	271.0	16	7 winter storms, 3 floods, 3 wildfires, 2 droughts, 1 windstorm
Mozambique	442.0	3,620	12.2	41	15 droughts, 14 floods, 5 windstorms, 5 cyclones, 1 slide, 1 famine
Namibia	1.1	2,870	0.0	8	7 droughts, 1 flood
Netherlands Antilles	17.1	2,740	0.6	2	2 hurricanes
New Caledonia	0.4	…	…	7	7 cyclones
Nicaragua	2,556.4	2,610	97.9	32	8 floods, 4 droughts, 4 volcanoes, 3 earthquakes, 3 wildfires, 4 storms
Niger	14.1	2,180	0.6	21	10 droughts, 7 floods, 3 insect infestations, 1 windstorm
Papua New Guinea	582.6	2,930	19.9	33	10 earthquakes, 6 volcanoes, 5 slides, 5 floods, 3 droughts
Rwanda	…	1,740	…	9	4 floods, 4 droughts, 1 earthquake
Samoa	619.5	260	238.3	6	3 cyclones, 1 windstorm, 1 wildfire, 1 flood
São Tomé and Príncipe	…	50	…	2	2 droughts
Seychelles	1.8	700	0.3	2	1 flood, 1 tropical storm
Sierra Leone	9.9	780	1.3	4	3 windstorms, 1 flood
Solomon Islands	29.4	320	9.2	12	6 cyclones, 2 earthquakes, 2 droughts, 1 tsunami, 1 windstorm
St. Kitts and Nevis	327.8	360	91.1	7	6 hurricanes, 1 flood
St. Lucia	1,552.2	660	235.2	8	4 hurricanes, 2 tropical storms, 1 windstorm, 1 slide
St. Vincent and the Grenadines	46.3	360	12.9	9	4 hurricanes, 4 floods, 1 volcano
Swaziland	85.8	1,200	7.2	10	8 droughts, 1 cyclone, 1 flood
Tajikistan	706.3	1,210	58.4	25	12 floods, 5 slides, 3 earthquakes, 2 droughts, 2 windstorms
Togo	…	1,360	…	6	4 floods, 2 droughts
Tonga	112.6	140	80.4	9	7 cyclones, 1 windstorm, 1 earthquake
Vanuatu	304.3	230	132.3	27	14 cyclones, 8 earthquakes, 2 windstorms, 1 slide, 1 volcano
Zambia	22.7	3,760	0.6	14	7 droughts, 5 floods, 2 insect infestations

Source: Center for Research on Epidemiology of Disasters (CRED) and Office of Foreign Disaster Assistance (OFDA), EM-DAT.
Note: Small countries are defined as those with GDP below $5 billion in 2002. Disasters in EM-DAT are defined as those natural disasters that have caused 10 or more fatalities, affected 100 or more people, led to an appeal for international assistance, or resulted in a declaration of a state of emergency. The data are based on reports sent to CRED and compiled by external organizations such as the various UN organizations, country governments, aid-disbursing agencies, and reinsurance companies.

Table 7. Output Growth and Trading Partners' Growth, 1970–2002

	Slope Coefficient	R^2
Advanced economies (49)		
Mean	0.886	0.281
Median	0.914	0.266
Emerging market countries (28)		
Mean	0.805	0.139
Median	0.841	0.068
Developing economies (23)		
Mean	0.542	0.084
Median	0.517	0.043

Sources: IMF, *International Financial Statistics* and *Direction of Trade Statistics*.

Note: The regressions use annual data for 1970–2002, when available. Countries with fewer than 20 observations are not considered. The definition of advanced economies is derived from the IMF's *World Economic Outlook*. The set of emerging market countries is the union of those defined as such by the International Finance Corporation, *Global Stock Market Factbook 2000*, and the JPMorgan Emerging Market Bond Index Global. The remaining countries are included in the set of developing countries. The number of countries in each group is reported in parentheses.

Changes in Total Imports by Main Trading Partners

As noted above, many countries would not derive major insurance benefits from instruments hedging specific risks, such as natural disasters or changes in commodity prices. For these countries, especially highly open economies, changes in total imports or output by main trading partners might constitute an important determinant of economic performance. It is therefore worth considering whether it would be desirable to let a country's bond repayments depend on an index of total imports by the country's main trading partners.

Regressions of individual countries' annual output growth on trade-weighted partner growth may help gauge the extent to which indexation to partner growth might stabilize the debt-to-GDP ratio for the various countries (Table 7).[10] For many advanced economies, output growth is clearly related to developments in partner countries. The relationship is more tenuous—with lower average R^2 coefficients—for emerging market countries and developing countries.[11] A possible interpretation of this finding is that advanced countries tend to export services and manu-

factures with a relatively high technological content, for which demand shocks are more relevant; by contrast, emerging market countries and developing countries tend to export commodities, for which supply shocks are more relevant, and manufactures with lower technological content, for which demand might increase when the advanced economies experience low growth and redirect their demand toward cheaper goods. Developments in trading partners' output growth are found to be a key determinant of economic growth also over longer time horizons: using five-year panel regressions, Arora and Vamvakidis (2004) find that a 1 percentage point increase in trading partners' growth raises a country's growth rate by as much as 0.8 percentage points, with the effect being somewhat stronger in more open economies.

In sum, several countries would derive considerable benefits from insurance or indexation to real variables largely beyond the control of the national authorities, such as natural disasters, commodity prices, or trading-partner output growth. Nevertheless, many countries, including several among the main emerging markets, seem unlikely to derive significant benefits from such insurance or indexation.

Real Variables Partially Within the Control of the Country's Authorities

Indexing to broader indicators of a country's economic performance would provide a closer match to its ability to repay. The closest indicators would be GDP or exports; related indicators such as industrial production or electricity consumption could also be

---

[10]Trading-partner output growth is constructed as a weighted average of output growth for all trading partners for which data are available. For year t, the weights are computed as the share of exports to each country and are 11-year moving averages centered on year t.

[11]Similarly, the relationship is statistically significant in 18 out of 23 advanced economies, but there are only 9 out of 28 emerging market countries and 9 out of 49 developing countries for which data are available for at least 20 years.

considered. The macroeconomic benefits that borrowing countries might derive from real indexation can be illustrated by a number of simple numerical examples, which, for the sake of brevity, are presented here for the case of GDP.

A Simple Example

Consider the case of a country whose real GDP has been growing for many years at 3 percent and it is expected to continue doing so. Assume that this country can issue regular, plain vanilla bonds at, say, 7 percent interest. That country could consider issuing a dollar-denominated, floating-rate bond with a coupon rate that varies according to the performance of the domestic economy. Specifically, the coupon rate could equal

$$coupon_t = \max\,[r + (g_t - \bar{g}),\, 0], \qquad (1)$$

where

g_t = actual growth rate of GDP,

$\bar{g}$ = baseline growth rate of GDP,

and

r = 7 percent.

The baseline growth rate of GDP is agreed upon by the contracting parties prior to the bonds' issue: in this case, 3 percent could be a reasonable baseline. The coupon rate might be expected to include a small insurance premium in addition to the 7 percent charged for plain vanilla bonds, but this insurance premium is set to zero in this example. Yearly coupon payments will be reduced by 1 percentage point for every percentage point by which real GDP growth falls short of its 3 percent trend—but the coupon has a minimum of zero. In years when growth turns out to be 1 percent, the coupon will be 5 percent. In years when growth turns out to be 5 percent, the coupon will be 9 percent.

This exercise and those that follow are based on the relatively simple formula above. Continuity—with small changes in realized growth resulting in small changes in coupon payments—seems desirable to minimize incentives to misreport. The need for symmetry—with the coupon varying in proportion to the gap between actual and baseline GDP growth on both the upside and the downside—may be a more open question. Many institutional bond investors are required to hold assets that pay a positive interest rate, suggesting the need for a zero or positive minimum for the coupon rate. Borrowers might prefer to include a cap on coupon payments, which is omitted in this example. The link from the growth rate to coupon payments could follow more complicated formulas, but simplicity is likely to be crucial in helping sell this type of instrument. In-

dexation could apply to the principal, but it seems preferable to apply it to the coupon, because this yields interest savings during times of weak economic growth, thereby reducing the need for fiscal policies to be procyclical. At any rate, mutual agreement between borrowers and lenders would seem the most natural way of determining the exact form of the contract.

When GDP growth turns out lower than usual, debt payments due will also be lower than in the absence of indexation, helping maintain the debt-to-GDP ratio at sustainable levels, and avoiding what could be a costly and politically difficult adjustment in the primary balance at a time of weak economic performance. Conversely, when GDP growth turns out higher than usual, the country will pay more than it would have without indexation, thus reducing its debt-to-GDP ratio less than it would have otherwise. In sum, this insurance scheme keeps the debt-to-GDP ratio within a narrower range. For this insurance, the borrowing country will pay a small premium above the interest rate that it would ordinarily be charged.

Using the specific form of the contract in (1), the following example may be considered. Suppose that beginning in 1990, half of the total government debt of Mexico and Argentina consisted of these GDP-indexed bonds. And suppose that the average growth rate over the 20 years prior to the beginning of the contract is chosen as the baseline growth rate. For the purpose of this example, assume that the composition of the debt has no impact on the behavior of any of the other variables in the economy: variables such as the GDP growth rate and the overall deficit behave exactly as they did in 1991–2002. What coupon rates would have been paid on the bonds, and what would have been the interest savings (or extra costs) for these two countries?

Mexico (Figure 11, top panel) grew relatively rapidly in the 20 years prior to 1990, by 4.4 percent on average, compared to about 3 percent in 1991–2002. This would have resulted in an average coupon rate of 5.9 percent compared to the expected 7 percent. In good years, Mexico would have paid higher-than-average coupon rates. However, during the Tequila crisis of 1995, when output contracted by more than 6 percent, the coupon rate would have fallen to its minimum of zero. Mexico would have obtained a large reduction in the interest bill, leaving more room to avoid procyclical fiscal measures. Large interest savings would also have applied during the sudden slowdown of 2001–02.

In Argentina (Figure 11, lower panel), growth over the 20 years prior to 1990 averaged only 0.9 percent per year. In 1991–2002, despite two major crises, the average growth rate rose to 2.3 percent. This would have resulted in coupon rates of 8.8 per-

Figure 11. Interest Savings over the Economic Cycle

(Interest bill savings as percent of GDP, left scale; Coupon and GDP growth rates in percent, right scale)

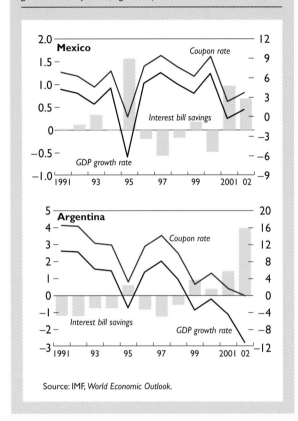

Source: IMF, *World Economic Outlook.*

higher primary surplus (lower primary spending and higher taxes) than without indexation. Thus GDP indexation of bond repayments tends to make for smoother paths of the primary surplus, taxes, and primary spending, over the cycle. The advantages could be large for both emerging market countries and advanced economies (Box 7).

While this paper focuses on emerging market countries, GDP indexation could also help advanced economies to avoid procyclical fiscal policies, in particular where the government faces constraints on its deficit level. The constraints could arise from legal or constitutional provisions (as for some of the U.S. states) or a concerted policy commitment such as the Stability and Growth Pact of the European Union. To gauge the benefits of GDP-indexed bonds for advanced economies, Borensztein and Mauro (2004) consider what would have happened to the debts, total deficits, and primary deficits of some of the European Monetary Union (EMU) countries had they been subject to a 3 percent of GDP limit on the fiscal deficit beginning in 1980, and then simulate what would have happened to their primary deficits had the debt been indexed to GDP. Adjusting the primary balance to meet the 3 percent total deficit ceiling would have significantly curbed the ability of some of these countries to conduct countercyclical fiscal policy. Growth-indexed debt, however, would have largely offset the impact of the deficit ceiling, helping preserve the countercyclicality of fiscal policy.

Having argued that GDP-indexed bonds might provide substantial insurance benefits, it remains to be shown whether the insurance premium countries might expect to pay would be sufficiently small for the insurance to be attractive to them.

cent on average. The coupon rate would have fallen sharply in 1995 (Tequila crisis) and again beginning in 1999 (Brazil crisis), though it would have hit the minimum of zero only in 2002. Interestingly, Argentina defaulted on foreign debt in 2002 and actually did not make any interest payments in that year. Argentina would have made roughly no net savings on its interest bill: it would have paid higher-than-average coupon rates in the years of rapid growth (the early 1990s), but would have made sizable savings in its interest bill since 1999.

Avoiding Procyclical Fiscal Policy

The example above illustrates how GDP indexation of bond repayments could reduce the need for countries to engage in procyclical fiscal policy. When GDP growth is below trend, the government will be able to have a lower primary surplus (higher primary spending and lower taxes) with indexation than without it; conversely, when GDP growth is above trend, the government will need to have a

Diversifiability of Growth Across Countries and the Insurance Premium

Pricing financial instruments that do not yet exist is a difficult task, but considerations loosely based on the Capital Asset Pricing Model (CAPM) suggest that the insurance premium on GDP-indexed bonds issued by emerging market countries would likely be small. In fact, income growth rates are not highly correlated with possible measures of a "world market portfolio," and the CAPM implies that only the systematic portion of risk is reflected in expected returns, because unsystematic risk can be diversified away by investors.[12]

---

[12]This is in line with studies that show large, unrealized gains from international risk sharing resulting from the relatively low correlation of income growth rates across countries, at a variety of horizons (Athanasoulis, Shiller, and van Wincoop, 1999).

Box 7. Benefits of GDP Indexation for Emerging Markets and Advanced Economies

How much additional room would countries have had for countercyclical fiscal policy if their debt had been indexed to GDP at the beginning of the 1990s? To address that question, a simple exercise is conducted for 20 advanced economies and 25 emerging market countries. For each country, it is assumed that, in 1991, the entire debt stock was indexed to GDP; each year, the interest rate on the entire debt under the indexed contract would equal the implied interest rate (from the interest bill and the previous year's debt stock) observed in the actual data plus an indexation term equal to the difference between actual growth and baseline growth (with a minimum of zero); the baseline growth in the contract was the average growth rate in 1980–2001, which could be viewed as resulting from a mix of adaptive expectations and perfect foresight; and total deficits (and thus the total debt path)

and economic growth were exactly as observed during the simulation period. Then it is estimated what the primary balance would have been with indexation in 1992–2001, and the resulting correlation between the primary balance and the GDP growth rate—a summary measure of the government's ability to conduct countercyclical fiscal policy. (For example, if primary spending is more expansionary during recessions, that correlation will be higher.) This correlation is then compared to the same measure based upon actual data.

The correlation between the primary balance and the GDP growth rate would have been substantially higher with indexation than it was in the actual data, and the increase in correlation would have been slightly more pronounced for emerging market countries than it would for advanced economies (see the table).

Correlation Between Primary Balance and Real GDP Growth

	Emerging Markets		Advanced Economies	
	Without indexation	With indexation	Without indexation	With indexation
Mean	0.30	0.77	0.40	0.64
Median	0.37	0.80	0.45	0.74

Sources: OECD, Analytical database; and IMF, *International Financial Statistics*, *Government Finance Statistics*, and Country Reports.

Note: Emerging market countries include Argentina, Brazil, Bulgaria, Chile, China, Colombia, Côte d'Ivoire, Ecuador, Hungary, India, Indonesia, Korea, Lebanon, Malaysia, Mexico, Morocco, Nigeria, Pakistan, Peru, Philippines, Poland, South Africa, Turkey, Uruguay, and Venezuela. Advanced economies include Australia, Austria, Belgium, Canada, Denmark, Finland, France, Germany, Iceland, Ireland, Italy, Japan, Luxembourg, Netherlands, New Zealand, Norway, Spain, Sweden, United Kingdom, and United States.

Simple regressions of individual countries' GDP growth rates on various proxies for the return on the "world market portfolio" (including world real stock returns, U.S. real stock returns, world GDP growth, and U.S. GDP growth) yield relatively low R^2 coefficients.[13] For emerging market countries, the highest R^2 coefficient is 0.20 (Russia) using world stock returns; beta coefficients range from –0.6 (Bulgaria) to 0.43 (Russia), with an unweighted average of 0.032 (Borensztein and Mauro, 2004). Comovement across countries is somewhat higher for advanced countries, and marginally lower for developing countries.

To illustrate the implications of the equation above for the pricing of GDP-indexed bonds, the following example assumes that the relevant portfolio

for investors is the world stock market, the risk-free rate of return is 3 percent, the expected return on the market portfolio is 8 percent and, taking the case of Mexico from the (unreported) individual country regressions, that the β of the country's growth rate with respect to the return on the world stock market is 0.072. Then, the indexation premium will be $(8 - 3) \times 0.072$, that is, 0.36 percentage point a year—fairly small compared with the spreads often observed in emerging markets. This premium is in excess of the rate that the country pays on plain vanilla bonds, that is, it is in addition to the premium that compensates for default risk. It is likely, however, that default risk would decline significantly if a country were to convert a large portion of its debt into indexed bonds such as these. For simplicity, the above assumes that the default risk is uncorrelated with the GDP growth risk. The appeal of indexed bonds is even greater when this assumption is relaxed, letting default risk rise when growth falls.

---

[13]The sample period is 1970–2001. The broad findings are unchanged, focusing on subperiods that might be viewed as characterized by greater financial and trade globalization or more frequent emerging market crises.

Obstacles for Variables Partly Within the Control of the Government

Despite its potential advantages, real indexation has been used in practice only in a limited number of cases (Box 8). If such advantages were really significant, as the analysis above suggests, why has real indexation not been more widespread? Part of the answer, of course, is that creating markets for new financial instruments is never easy, as argued in Section II. However, indexation to real variables that are partly within the control of the government, such as GDP, presents an additional set of practical and conceptual obstacles that are discussed below.

- *Possibility of lower incentives for growth-promoting policies.* Bonds indexed to variables that are partly affected by government policies could reduce the authorities' incentives to pursue growth-promoting policies. The extent to which a government (whether benevolent or kleptocratic) would—for a number of years—pursue less growth-oriented policies with indexed bonds than it would with standard bonds (on which it could default) is an open question, but investors might reasonably be concerned about that possibility.

- *Potential misreporting.* When repayments are linked to economic indicators produced by the debtor country, the authorities might be tempted to tamper with the measurement of those indicators. How strong the temptation would be, and whether the authorities would place their reputation (and possibly market access) at stake are also open questions.[14] Nevertheless, the potential for misreporting could make investors reluctant to hold instruments of this type. Of course, it is high growth rather than low growth that is typically considered a success and gets politicians reelected, but the incentives might be reversed if the new instruments were to constitute a large fraction of a country's external debt.

- *Data revisions.* Even for advanced countries, revisions compared with initial data releases for variables such as GDP can be substantial. Investors might perceive potential data revisions as an unwelcome source of uncertainty, and might be concerned about the possibility that debtor countries might use the revisions opportunistically to reduce repayments.

- *Lags.* The benefits of real indexation in reducing the procyclicality of fiscal policy depend on whether repayments are linked to variables that truly reflect the current state of the economy. Although the state of the economic cycle tends to persist in time and GDP data become available with only a few months' delay in many countries, debtor countries might be concerned about linking repayments to macroeconomic indicators that, in practice, become available with significant lags.

- *High volatility of returns.* While many international investors already invest in emerging market financial instruments with very volatile returns, such as stocks, some bond investors might be reluctant to accept the additional volatility of returns resulting from the variable coupon payments associated with real indexation. Moreover, many institutional investors may be prevented from doing so by the constraints placed on the range of assets that they are allowed to invest in.

- *Complexity and difficulty in pricing.* While some financial market players thrive on dealing with and pricing complicated financial instruments, many investors, especially bond investors, are often reluctant to buy instruments that are difficult to understand and price. Indeed, for bond investors in particular, there appears to be a trend away from complex instruments toward simple bonds, as shown by several swaps to retire Brady bonds, and a decline in the prominence of floating-rate bonds. While a generally accepted pricing formula does not seem to be necessary for a market to operate, lack of a well-established pricing model for GDP-indexed bonds might hamper their acceptance by investors. Indeed, if investors were to apply a very high discount rate to future uncertain payments, borrowing countries would find GDP-indexed bonds too costly to be issued.

- *Politicians' short horizons.* As real indexation would have a significant impact only for relatively long-term bonds, politicians currently in power—given their short horizons—might be reluctant to pay an insurance premium today in exchange for benefits that might only be reaped by their successors.

- *Inability to recall the bonds.* Real indexation is unlikely to be consistent with the callability of bonds. Suppose that a GDP-indexed bond were callable: should GDP growth turn out better than expected, the interest rate faced by the country on standard bonds would presumably fall (because the country would now look more solvent); the borrower would then have an incentive to recall

---

[14]It is not clear whether episodes of cheating on the data would necessarily kill a market: stock markets, for example, have survived many scandals of this type. Misreporting is always a possibility that investors are aware of, and it is presumably reflected in asset prices.

Box 8. Previous Examples of Indexation to Real Variables

A handful of emerging market countries have already issued bonds with elements of real indexation: Mexico has issued bonds indexed to oil prices; and various Brady bonds issued by Mexico, Nigeria, Uruguay, and Venezuela to commercial banks in exchange for defaulted loans in the early 1990s were issued with value recovery rights (VRRs) that were designed to provide additional payments in the event of an increase in prices of commodities such as oil. However, the indexation formulas were exceedingly complex, and the characteristics of each country's formulas differed widely. Moreover, there were restrictions on the tradability of the bonds and the detachability of the VRRs (http://www.emta.org/ndevelop/primer.pdf). Loans combined with protection (through swaps) from commodity price fluctuations have also been made available by the World Bank to member countries, beginning in September 1999, though interest has thus far been limited.

Costa Rica, Bulgaria, and Bosnia and Herzegovina have issued bonds containing an element of indexation to GDP. These bonds, which were issued as part of Brady restructuring agreements, contain clauses or warrants (value recovery rights) that increase the payoff to bondholders if GDP (or GDP per capita) of the debtor country rises above a certain level. In the case of Bulgaria, the bonds provided for a GDP "kicker" such that, once real GDP exceeds 125 percent of its 1993 level, creditors will be entitled to an additional 0.5 percent in interest for every 1 percent of real GDP growth in the year prior to interest payment. At the same time, these bonds were callable by the issuer and even at the time of issue it was widely expected that Bulgaria would repay the principal and refinance it, should the kicker appear likely to be triggered by rapid economic growth. Indeed, Bulgaria has already swapped a portion of its indexed bonds for newly issued, nonindexed bonds. In any case, indexed bonds are very much exceptions, and, in the few instances when they have been

issued, the indexation clause was set so far "out of the money" that it was unlikely ever to be triggered.

Going beyond sovereigns, one set of bonds (for a few hundred million dollars and a maturity of four to six years) recently restructured by the city of Buenos Aires includes indexation of principal repayments to the city's revenues. This seems quite close to the notion of equity for a public entity (the proceeds from the right to collect taxes). Indexation to revenues, however, would seem unlikely to gain widespread acceptance, owing to reduced incentives to collect revenues.

Finally, moving away from bonds and toward pure claims to the indexation component, a market for derivatives on indicators of real economic activity has recently been developed. In September 2002, Goldman Sachs and Deutsche Bank successfully completed the first-ever parimutuel auctions of economic derivatives—specifically, options on the U.S. Bureau of Labor Statistics release of change in U.S. Nonfarm Payroll data for September 2002 (www.longitude.com/html/news_oct04_2002.html). In April 2003, the same firms hosted pari-mutuel auctions for three- and six-month options on the European Harmonized Index of Consumer Prices (*Risk Magazine*, March 2003). (See also Baron and Lange, 2003.)

While there are no precedents of IFIs linking repayments to measures of economic activity, the IFIs have—in exceptional cases—made loan disbursements explicitly conditional on economic activity. The IMF's Stand-By Arrangement with Mexico in 1986 included a growth contingency such that, should GDP growth fall below a benchmark level, the authorities would be allowed to implement an additional public investment program, financed by additional loans from the World Bank and commercial banks. The growth contingency mechanism was activated in 1988 (Boughton, 2001, pp. 441–50). The use of adjustors—especially for changes in commodity prices—in IMF programs also plays a similar role.

---

the indexed bonds and issue plain vanilla bonds at a lower interest rate. At present, less than 5 percent of all emerging market bonds are effectively callable. However, the ability to recall a bond is another important form of insurance—in this case, against fluctuations in interest rates. Therefore, the appeal of GDP-indexed bonds may depend on the relative importance of uncertainty over interest rates and uncertainty over GDP growth.

The importance of such obstacles was assessed through a systematic survey of market participants conducted by IMF researchers in collaboration with the Emerging Markets Traders Association (EMTA) and the Emerging Markets Creditors Association (EMCA). Respondents identified liquidity and the potential for mismeasurement of GDP as the key obstacles in using growth-linked instruments. The survey and the results are described in further detail in the appendix.

Steps to Foster Acceptance

Overcoming many of the obstacles that might make it difficult for real indexation to emerge requires credibility, which is ultimately to be provided by the potential issuers. Nevertheless, a number of additional steps could be considered if these bonds are deemed useful:

- *Improving the quality and timeliness of the data.* Ensuring that the macroeconomic indicators accurately reflect the state of the economy is crucial for countries to reap the full benefits of real indexation. This is especially important to ensure that indexation acts as an accurate "automatic stabilizer."

- *Ensuring the integrity of the data.* Investors' main concern may be that errors or revisions could be used opportunistically in order to reduce debt payments. While the existence of substantial markets for CPI-indexed bonds in many countries suggests that data integrity issues are not insurmountable, it may be more difficult to accurately estimate real GDP than consumer prices. To overcome these problems, the importance of macroeconomic indicators could be reemphasized in the current drive toward increased transparency and improved data quality, which involves efforts such as the Reports on the Observance of Standards and Codes (ROSCs).[15] Governments could likewise strive to guarantee the independence of statistical agencies. Alternatively, GDP-linked contracts could be based on indicators produced by independent sources not affiliated with the government, or the quality of the data could be assessed by independent reviewers.[16]

- *Drafting a sample indexation clause.* As in the case of collective action clauses, a sample indexation clause could be designed for possible inclusion in bond contracts. To avoid uncertainty and scope for opportunistic tampering with the data, such a clause could provide a clear definition of the variables determining payments due. The definition could include the agency responsible for producing the data, the time of data release and coupon payment, and a statement that methodological changes would not be taken into consideration for the purposes of determining payments due. Alternatively, an outside party could vet that any methodological change stemmed from purely technical motives. A clear method for dealing with revisions could also be established. One possibility would be to state that data revisions would be ignored, and to establish that coupon payments for each given date would be based on GDP as estimated on a predetermined date.

- *Drawing on commitment to sound policies.* Countries whose commitment to sound policies is underpinned by rules or formal agreements (e.g., the Stability and Growth Pact) might be especially good candidates for real indexation. In

fact, not only would such countries be more likely to derive benefits from less procyclical fiscal policies but they would also find it easier to persuade markets that real indexation would not result in inappropriate policies.

- *Building on existing systems of peer monitoring of data.* Countries that have already shown they can agree on common statistical standards to define and monitor GDP data for an important purpose (such as European countries involved in the Maastricht convergence process and the Stability and Growth Pact) might find it relatively easy to persuade markets of the reliability of their macroeconomic data.

- *Meeting demand by institutional investors.* Opportunities to place nonstandard bonds are sometimes created by the investment objectives of institutional investors. For example, inflation-indexed bonds are often considered to be attractive to private pension funds. Some advanced economies' public pension systems de facto tend to index pension benefits to GDP. Private pension plans, which may seek returns close to that benchmark, might therefore be interested in investing in GDP-indexed bonds issued by the government.

Real Indexation: Which Variables for Which Countries?

Which variables are more likely to make real indexation attractive to both borrowing countries and international investors? Individual country characteristics are most relevant in determining borrowers' interest. Tailor-made contracts could be provided over the counter, especially to small countries, by global private financial institutions. However, some degree of standardization of contracts across countries would be key for the emergence of a dedicated class of traders and investors, and would be especially important for the creation of an active and liquid secondary market on an organized exchange.

In considering which variables or set of variables they could index to, individual countries would seek to identify the variables that would best help preserve debt sustainability while attracting interest on the part of international investors. In choosing among variables that are largely outside the control of the authorities, the main criterion is likely to be which contingency best adjusts the value of debt to the country's repayment capacity. Insurance against natural disasters or changes in commodity prices may be desirable for a number of countries, including several small developing countries and those emerging market countries whose production struc-

---

[15]On best practices with respect to data revisions, see Carson, Khawaja, and Morrison (2004).

[16]Payments arising from inflation-indexed securities issued by Brazil's federal government are based upon an inflation measure produced by the Getúlio Vargas Foundation.

tures rely on one or a few commodities. For larger and more diversified economies at a higher stage of economic development, indexing to trading-partner output growth is more likely to be relevant.

When considering variables that are partly within the control of the authorities, considerations related to the credibility of policies and measurement are likely to weigh more heavily. While the exercises above have considered the case of GDP indexation, the volume of exports is also a relevant measure of economic performance and external repayment capacity, and the debt-to-exports ratio is a closely watched indicator. Indeed, for many developing countries, data on exports might well be more reliable than data on GDP. At the same time, govern-ment policies may affect trade openness more directly than they affect GDP, and indexation to a country's overall exports might reduce incentives to undertake policies promoting trade openness. Other alternatives include industrial production or electricity consumption, which in some countries are highly correlated with GDP and yet possibly harder to tamper with than GDP data. However, the extent to which these variables represent good proxies for overall economic activity varies widely across countries. All in all, GDP—the most comprehensive and generally accepted measure of a country's income—would seem the most natural candidate if the bonds of many different countries were to be indexed to the same economic variable.

VI Past and Future of Innovation in Sovereign Borrowing

As argued in Section II, several obstacles to financial innovation involve the need to coordinate the actions of many economic agents. This suggests that financial innovation may be expected to take place in discrete steps, rather than gradually, which at times are hard to predict. Indeed, financial innovation in practice turns out to look like a rather haphazard process. New financial instruments do not seem to be adopted as the end-product of a systematic search, or a gradual evolution leading to superior forms of finance. Instead, innovation seems to result from historical accident, a constellation of special circumstances, or strong intervention on the part of policymakers.[1]

Financial Innovation in Sovereign Borrowing: A Haphazard Process

While the bulk of sovereign borrowing has historically taken the form of plain vanilla debt, sovereign borrowers have displayed considerable creativity over the years. In 1782, the State of Virginia issued bonds linked to the price of land and slaves. In 1863, the Confederate States of America issued "cotton" bonds payable in pounds sterling or French francs but convertible into cotton at a predetermined price. This was an excellent hedge: if cotton prices went up, higher value would be transferred from the borrower to the lender—as investors requested payment in the form of cotton—just as revenues rose for the Confederate States, a major cotton producer (Barone and Masera, 1997). In the pre–World War I era of bond finance, it was common for the emerging market countries of the day to issue bonds simultaneously in more than one major exchange, with coupons payable in any one of a few currencies, at the discretion of the investor. For example, in 1913 China issued a bond with coupons payable in sterling, rubles, marks, francs, or yen (Flandreau and Sussman, 2002). "Gold

clauses," effectively indexing payments to the price of gold, were widespread in the United States in the nineteenth century through 1933 (Kroszner, 1999).

Despite such creativity, innovations in sovereign borrowing have been limited, and regularities in their timing and form are hard to discern on the basis of macroeconomic fundamentals. Leadership and intervention on the part of the official sector often underlie the timing and nature of financial innovation. This point may be illustrated by referring to three historical experiences: first, the history of the introduction of inflation-indexed bonds in a variety of countries; second, the episode of syndicated bank loans in the 1970s; and third, the recent introduction of collective action clauses.

- *Inflation-indexed bonds.* The case for inflation-indexed bonds has been made at various stages during the past couple of centuries by many of the leading economists of their day (Barone and Masera, 1997). Yet, countries' experiences differ widely on the timing and circumstances under which they introduced inflation-indexed bonds (Table 8). A few sovereigns began issuing inflation-indexed bonds several decades ago; others have done so more recently; the vast majority have never issued indexed bonds at all. There does not appear to be much association between country characteristics and the introduction of inflation-indexed bonds. Countries that have issued indexed debt are at various stages of development, including both advanced economies and emerging market countries. (Developing countries with relatively limited statistical capacity have not issued such bonds.) While some countries, such as Brazil, Israel, and the United Kingdom, began issuing inflation-indexed bonds during periods of high inflation, others have experienced high inflation without resorting to these bonds, and several, such as Canada, Sweden, and the United States, began issuing indexed bonds during periods of low inflation. Moreover, for inflation-prone countries, indexed bonds are not necessarily issued in the proximity of inflation peaks. Similarly, while

---

Note: The author of this section and the next is Paolo Mauro.

[1]Borensztein and Mauro (2004) provide greater detail and further evidence on the issues addressed in this section.

Table 8. Introduction of Inflation-Indexed Securities by Sovereigns

	Period of Issue	Average CPI Inflation Rate in Three Years Prior to Introduction (In percent)	Indexed Public Debt Outstanding in 1999	
			In millions of U.S. dollars	In percent of total government debt
Argentina	1972–1989	18.6	0	0
Australia	1985–1988	8.4	...	...
	1993–	3.8	27,860	29.5
Brazil	1964–	...	45,291	19.6
Canada	1991–	4.6	6,636	1.5
Chile	1956–	39.6	14,960	62.0
Colombia	1967–	13.7	4,949[1]	13.2[1]
Czech Republic	1997–	9.3	150	1.7
Finland	1945–	...	0.7	0
France	1998–	1.7	3,994	0.6
Greece	1997–	7.6	197	0.2
Hungary	1995–	23.2	394	3
Iceland	1955–	4.3	494[2]	11.5[2]
India	...	...	166	0.2
Ireland	1983–	18.6	260	1.1
Israel	1955–	32.7	79,037	80.2
Italy	1983[3]	18.5	0	0
	2003[4]	2.2	11,938	0.9
Japan	2004[5]	−0.6	900	0.0[6]
Mexico	1989–	110.7	2,528	8.4
New Zealand	1977–1984	14.2	...	...
	1994–	1.4	361	2.3
Norway	1982–	9.8	30	0.1
Poland	1992–2000	292.2	0[7]	0.0[7]
Sweden	1952[3]	8.2	...	...
	1994–	5.4	15,475	12.5
Turkey	1994–	80.8	8,561	24.3
United Kingdom	1975–[8]	10.7	...	...
United Kingdom	1981–	13.2	55,288	12
United States	1997–	2.8	57,014	0.8

Sources: Campbell and Shiller (1996); Kopcke and Kimball (1999); Price (1997); Deacon and Derry (1998); official websites of country authorities; and IMF staff estimates.

[1]January 2003.

[2]February 2003.

[3]Only one issue of inflation-indexed bonds.

[4]One issue in September 2003, indexed to euro area inflation measured by Eurostat.

[5]One issue in March 2004.

[6]From March 2004.

[7]From April 2000.

[8]Index-linked national savings certificates.

some countries introduced inflation-indexed bonds around the time they promoted the use of private pension plans, there is no simple relationship with pension system or reform.

• *Syndicated bank loans.* One reading of history is that the largest innovation in how emerging markets countries have financed themselves during the past two centuries—namely, the temporary switch to syndicated bank loans in the 1970s—largely owed to official encouragement and implicit guarantees. Indeed, bond issues, now the predominant form of financing for emerging markets, have historically been the norm: financial flows to emerging markets took this form almost exclusively during the first golden era of global financial integration, until World War I brought such flows to an end (Bordo, Eichengreen, and Kim, 1998; Mauro, Sussman, and Yafeh, 2002). When international capital started flowing again toward emerging markets, in the aftermath of the first oil price shock, it did so in the form of syndicated bank loans. Why did savings by residents of oil-rich countries ultimately make their way to oil-importing emerging markets through banks in advanced economies rather than directly through bonds? Official encouragement and implicit guarantees of bank lending by the advanced economies led oil-rich country residents to place their savings primarily in a handful of the largest and most prestigious banks in the advanced economies. In turn, these banks found it profitable to on-lend such funds to emerging markets—at least until the debt crisis struck in the early 1980s. The return to bonds in the 1990s through the Brady deals of course also involved considerable intervention and subsidies on the part of the official sector.

• *Collective action clauses.* Finally, collective action clauses (CACs) had failed to emerge in New York law contracts until recently, even though the case for their introduction had been made for a number of years as part of the debate on reforming the international financial architecture. Once the international community mustered sufficient consensus about the desirability of CACs, they were adopted in sovereign bonds issued by several countries within a few months.[2] This is one example of how innovation may take place in the context of international coordination.

Road Maps for Future Innovation

Financial innovation in sovereign markets seems to be a somewhat haphazard process, and many beneficial financial innovations require intervention to be successful. Some of the instruments described in this paper seem to have desirable properties, and

with some improvement in statistical resources and credibility of data and policies, they might attract investors' interest.

While the process of financial innovation always faces significant hurdles, externalities would seem especially strong in the case of real indexation to variables that are partly within the control of the authorities. It would thus be difficult to develop a market for indexed bonds of this type through a gradual approach. A small initial issue would not be very attractive because it would do little to reduce the likelihood of a debt crisis. The holders of contingent debt would be implicitly subsidizing the holders of noncontingent debt. Two factors would substantially increase the chances of success: large scale would help both to reduce the probability of default significantly and to ensure sufficient liquidity on secondary markets; international coordination would help both to create a dedicated class of investors and to provide opportunities for risk diversification.

Two scenarios seem plausible for new types of bonds to be issued successfully:

• A large-scale launch by one country swapping a substantial proportion of the existing debt, possibly in the context of a debt restructuring. Indeed, historically, restructurings have provided opportunities for innovation: for example, value recovery rights (VRRs) were incorporated into Brady bond deals as investors looked for an upside opportunity to recoup previous losses. Other countries might follow, perhaps with large one-off swaps, not necessarily in the context of debt servicing difficulties.

• A launch of new bonds of the same type by several countries with some degree of—possibly informal—coordination. The recent introduction of collective action clauses by several issuers seems to constitute a precedent in this respect.

---

[2]See IMF (2003g).

VII   Conclusions

The debt structures of countries have an important influence on their economic performance and vulnerability to crises. In particular, excessive reliance by emerging market countries on short-term debt and foreign-currency debt exposes them to risks of rollover crises and sharp increases in the debt burden resulting from exchange rate changes. Of course, risky debt structures are often themselves symptoms of underlying institutional and policy weaknesses that need to be convincingly addressed. But beyond this, the paper has argued that there are valuable lessons to be extracted for improving sovereign debt structures from liability structures in the corporate sector. In particular, debt with different degrees of seniority, and instruments with equity-like features, could help to reduce the vulnerabilities inherent in current sovereign debt structures. Three key messages emerge from the analysis:

- First, credibility of fiscal and monetary policies is a central prerequisite to buttress investors' willingness to hold long-term local-currency bonds. Credibility, in turn, depends on both the quality of institutions and a reputation for sound policymaking. Without supporting reforms, building such a reputation can take many years, but the combination of macroeconomic stabilization with institutional and structural reforms can accelerate this process, as demonstrated by the experience of several emerging market countries, including Chile, Israel, Mexico, and Poland, in the last decade. Soon after bringing their inflation rates into the single digits and undertaking reforms of their monetary and fiscal frameworks, these countries successfully issued unindexed local-currency bonds with medium-term maturities. While initially relying on inflation-indexed bonds, which played a helpful and important role in the transition, most of these countries graduated to routinely issuing nonindexed long-term local-currency debt. This suggests that emerging market countries can improve their debt structures relatively quickly, as long as they show clear commitment to sound policies.

- Second, progress in overcoming the problem of debt dilution in the sovereign context could reduce the cost of borrowing and increase market access for low-debt countries, and help prevent crises that result from overborrowing and risky debt structures in high-debt countries. In the corporate context, debt dilution is addressed through methods that include debt covenants and explicit seniority. This paper has argued for consideration of analogous innovations in the sovereign context, in order to curb incentives for overborrowing, reduce costs of borrowing at low levels of debt, and limit the bias toward risky types of debt, such as short-term debt. This said, measures that reduce the scope for debt dilution are also likely to have some drawbacks: for example, making borrowing harder at high levels of debt may not always be desirable, especially if it exacerbates the risk of liquidity crises. In addition, some open questions remain, including the consequences of explicit legal seniority for crisis resolution and potential legal obstacles to the implementation of first-in-time seniority. While this cautions against making strong policy recommendations at the present time, the possible benefits of explicit seniority in the sovereign context seem to warrant further attention to the issue.

- Third, this paper has argued that instruments with equity-like features, which provide for lower payments in the event of adverse shocks and weak economic performance, could help sovereigns to improve debt sustainability and international risk sharing. Disaster insurance could benefit small countries prone to frequent natural disasters. Indexation to commodity prices might confer benefits for commodity-producing countries. GDP-indexed bonds would likely provide substantial insurance benefits to a broader range of countries, including the advanced economies and the main emerging market countries, though they present greater implementation challenges. In principle, GDP-indexed bonds could be issued relatively quickly, especially by countries with trusted and independent statistical offices. Whether these bonds would attract sufficient investor interest at reasonable cost to borrowing countries remains an open, empirical question. In particular, potential concerns of investors about complexities and difficulties in pricing would need to be addressed. Market acceptance and the requisite liquidity could be sought through international coordination or a large swap, possibly in the context of a restructuring. Countries could seek to ensure the independence of their statistical agencies, and technical assistance efforts could be stepped up in this area. More ambitiously, methods could be sought whereby outside parties could provide an independent view on whether countries' data are being systematically distorted.

The analysis in this paper suggests that progress in ameliorating debt structures could yield substantial benefits in economic performance and international risk sharing, while reducing the frequency of crises and the damage they entail. While sound policies remain a precondition for securing better sovereign debt structures, renewed attention to innovative structures that may have become possible as a result of the increased sophistication of financial markets could be well rewarded.

Appendix   Investors' Attitudes Toward Growth-Linked and Other Innovative Financial Instruments for Sovereign Borrowers: Results of a Survey

IMF researchers, in collaboration with the Emerging Markets Traders Association (EMTA) and the Emerging Markets Creditors Association (EMCA), conducted a survey study of market participants' attitudes toward innovation in emerging markets' debt instruments. The survey focused on growth-linked bonds, but also included questions about commodity-indexed and local-currency securities. The survey was distributed among the members of EMTA and EMCA, thus reaching a broad range of bond market participants, including participants from both the "buy side," such as asset managers and proprietary trading desk managers, and the "sell side," such as research strategists and analysts, as well as both "crossover" investors, who hold emerging market bonds only occasionally, in response to perceived profit opportunities, and emerging-market-dedicated investors.

Sample and Distribution Method

A link to the web-based survey was distributed via e-mail by EMTA and EMCA intermediaries to about 1,000 potential respondents at EMTA and 30 at EMCA, indicating that it had been designed by IMF researchers, who would not have access to respondent names or other individual information. Individual passwords allowed each respondent to fill out the survey only once.[1] An option was also provided to fill out the survey and return it via e-mail or fax, and a few respondents chose to do so.

Note: The authors of this appendix are Eduardo Borensztein and Paolo Mauro.

[1]This protected the integrity of the survey against the possibility of a single individual providing multiple entries. The selection of passwords for individual respondents was conducted by intermediaries. This information was not available to the researchers.

Research Strategy and Response Rate

In designing a survey of this type—to be sent without any incentives to busy financial market participants—there is a trade-off between length and the likely response rate. The design was somewhat more comprehensive and complex in both presentation of background information and seeking of potential answers. Growth-linked bonds in particular are more complicated than other existing instruments and needed to be presented clearly to financial market participants who were not familiar with them. Fewer responses based on a clearly formulated setup were considered to be preferable to more responses based on relatively limited information. Similarly, a key objective was considered to assess the relative importance of a fairly large number of potential obstacles to financial innovation.

Consequently, the number of responses turned out relatively low, at 28. This response rate should be viewed bearing in mind that the main questions covered uncharted territory and required considerable analysis by the respondents. An alternative interpretation of the low response rate is that potential respondents may have been generally dismissive of the idea of growth-linked bonds and decided that completing the survey was not worth their time. According to that interpretation, the results reported below would reflect selection bias in favor of growth-linked bonds, that is, they would provide an excessively optimistic picture of investors' views regarding growth-linked bonds.

Respondents were asked to indicate their profession and areas of expertise, for example, buy side versus sell side, or dedicated investor versus crossover investor. Despite its small size, the set of actual respondents spans a broad range of professions and areas of expertise. In presenting the results, we highlight any systematic differences in the responses that seem to depend on the type of respondent, though such results need to be interpreted with special caution owing to the small sample size.

Survey Results

Overall Attitudes Toward Growth-Linked Bonds

Questions 1 and 2 sought to assess respondents' overall attitudes toward growth-linked bonds. They presented two alternative designs for growth-linked bonds, and asked respondents to price such bonds.

Question 1 asked respondents to consider the case of an emerging market sovereign borrower ("EmergingLand," EL) that had successfully tapped international financial markets for a number of years, was currently not experiencing major problems, but whose bonds were trading at substantial spreads above U.S. treasuries. In the example, EL had experienced real GDP growth of 3 percent on average over the past 15 years, with a maximum of 7 percent, and a minimum of negative 8 percent; and average growth and volatility of GDP could be expected to be similar in the next decade. Respondents were asked to assume that 10-year eurobonds (U.S. dollar-denominated) issued by EL ("plain vanilla bonds," PV bonds) with a coupon of 7 percent currently trade at a spread of 400 basis points above U.S. treasuries. EL was said to be contemplating issuance of

a growth-indexed bond ("Growth Bond") with a 10-year maturity and with a coupon of 7 percent plus the difference between real GDP growth during that year and 3 percent. However, coupon payments were restricted to be non-negative:

$$\text{Coupon} = 7 \text{ percent} + (\text{real GDP growth} - 3 \text{ percent}), \text{ with a minimum of zero.}$$

Respondents were asked what premium they would require to hold a growth-linked bond rather than the plain vanilla bonds offering the same *expected* coupon payment. The growth-linked bond was designed to pay higher coupons in years when growth was higher than average, and lower coupons in years when growth was lower than average, with a minimum of zero. Respondents were given the following options: (1) spreads more than 50 basis points lower than PV bonds; (2) spreads 10–50 basis points lower than PV bonds; (3) same spreads as PV bonds; (4) spreads 10–50 basis points higher than PV bonds; (5) spreads 50–100 basis points higher than PV bonds; (6) spreads 100–200 basis points higher than PV bonds; (7) spreads 200–300 basis points higher than PV bonds; (8) spreads more than 300 basis points higher than PV bonds; and (9) unwilling to purchase regardless of the spreads.

As Figure A1 shows, there was a wide variety of answers: some respondents said that they would accept spreads that were lower or the same as those on PV bonds, whereas others said that they would be unwilling to purchase such bonds regardless of the spreads. The median answer was a premium of between 100 and 200 basis points. Buy-side respondents indicated somewhat higher premiums on average than sell-side respondents, as did "dedicated" emerging market investors compared to those who identified themselves as "crossover" investors.

Question 2 asked for the required premium when the growth-linked bond had a different specification, which ensured a minimum positive coupon payment regardless of the economic performance of the borrowing country at any given time. The yearly coupon had a minimum of 3.5 percent, and an extra payoff in years of positive growth, according to the following formula:

$$\text{Coupon} = 3.5 \text{ percent} + \text{real GDP growth, with a minimum of 3.5 percent.}$$

Respondents were told that this bond carried the same *expected* coupon as the bond in question 1. Respondents displayed greater propensity to hold the bond in question 2, with the mean premium over a plain vanilla bond being just over 100 basis points (Figure A2). This compares with a mean of just above 150 basis points for the bond in question 1. Again,

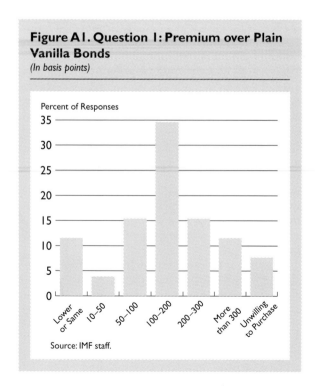

Figure A1. Question 1: Premium over Plain Vanilla Bonds
(In basis points)

Percent of Responses

Source: IMF staff.

sell-side participants and crossover investors appeared more willing to hold this bond than did buy-side market participants and dedicated investors.

Main Obstacles to Growth-Linked Bonds

Questions 3 and 4 sought to gauge the relative importance of a number of obstacles to the introduction of growth-linked bonds or, equivalently, the sources of premiums that investors would demand to hold growth-linked bonds rather than plain vanilla bonds.

Question 3 asked respondents whether any of a set of five hypothetical changes to the status quo would lead them to reduce the premiums they required to hold growth-linked bonds. The hypothetical changes as well as the corresponding mean and median answers are reported in Table A1: 1 is very important and would lead respondents to reduce the spreads by 50 basis points or more; 2 would lead respondents to reduce the spreads by 20–50 basis points; 3 would lead respondents to reduce the spreads by 10–20 basis points; and 4 is irrelevant.

As shown in Table A1, among the factors that would make respondents more willing to hold growth-linked bonds, they highlighted the issuance of a large volume of growth-linked bonds in the context of a debt restructuring operation and methods aimed at buttressing the integrity of the GDP data.

Question 4 was of a qualitative nature and asked respondents to consider which obstacles made them *reluctant* to hold growth-linked bonds. The potential obstacles as well as the corresponding mean and me-

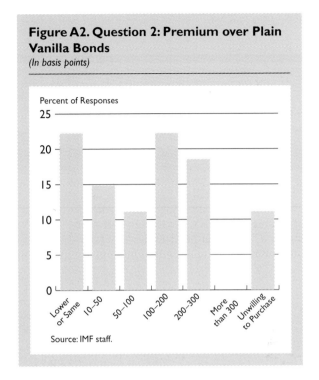

Figure A2. Question 2: Premium over Plain Vanilla Bonds
(In basis points)

Source: IMF staff.

dian answers are reported in Table A2: 1 is very important, 4 is not important.

Among the factors that made investors reluctant to hold growth-linked bonds, respondents pointed most often to uncertainty about future liquidity in markets for these bonds and concerns about the integrity of

Table A1. Question 3: Obstacles to Growth-Linked Bonds

Hypothetical Change	Mean	Median
The United States is planning to issue growth bonds at about the same time.	3.35	4
Five other major emerging market sovereigns are planning to issue growth bonds at about the same time.	2.95	3
A reliable economic consultancy firm announces it will provide free software with a formula for pricing growth bonds.	3.52	4
A well-respected international consortium reports a study showing that the GDP data provided by the country are reliable, and announces it will monitor GDP data quality annually.	2.78	3
Growth bonds covering at least 50 percent of the country's debt are issued in the context of a negotiated restructuring of EL's debt.	2.42	2

Table A2. Question 4: Obstacles to Growth-Linked Bonds

Potential Obstacle	Mean	Median
Uncertainty about future liquidity of growth bonds.	1.72	2
Complexity/difficulty in pricing.	2.23	2
Uncertainty about integrity of GDP data reported by EL.	1.73	1
Concern that EL will have fewer incentives to promote economic growth.	3.20	3
Variable coupon instead of fixed coupon.	2.91	3

Table A3. Question 5: Obstacles to Commodity-Indexed Bonds

Potential Obstacle	Mean	Median
It is too difficult to forecast commodity prices beyond three to five years.	2.54	3
You invest in many countries and only a few countries are heavily dependent on a single commodity. It is not worth your time to learn about commodity prices.	3.17	3
You are not interested in direct exposure to commodity price fluctuations, even if many of the countries you invest in are heavily dependent on commodities.	2.71	3
You are interested in exposure to commodity price fluctuations, but prefer to obtain it directly through forwards or futures linked to commodity prices.	2.36	2

Table A4. Question 6: Obstacles to Domestic-Currency Bonds

Potential Obstacle	Mean	Median
You are concerned about the possibility of a rise in inflation in EL.	1.91	1
You are concerned that EL's central bank could intervene in foreign exchange markets and pursue an unfavorable exchange rate close to the time when bond payments are due.	2.00	2
You are concerned about your ability to hedge exposure to EL's currency because of an illiquid NDF market.	2.04	2

GDP data that must be provided by the issuing sovereign. Those concerns were less important for dedicated emerging markets investors than they were for crossover investors. These results are consistent with the answers to question 2, and highlight the importance of both data reliability and market liquidity for potential investors in growth-linked bonds.

Commodity-Indexed Bonds

Question 5 sought to identify the reasons why commodity-indexed bonds have not been used more frequently. It asked respondents to consider the case of an emerging market that was heavily dependent on exports of a single commodity and sought to issue commodity-indexed bonds, that is, bonds whose return was indexed to the price of that commodity. Again, the question asked respondents to identify which potential obstacles made them *reluctant* to invest in commodity-indexed bonds. The potential obstacles as well as mean and median answers are reported in Table A3: 1 is very important, 4 is not important.

Respondents indicated that difficulties in forecasting commodity prices beyond a three-to-five-year horizon and a preference to obtain exposure to commodity prices directly through commodity derivatives made them reluctant to hold commodity-indexed bonds. In additional comments, some fund managers noted that they lacked a mandate to invest in commodities.

Domestic-Currency Bonds

Finally, respondents were asked to indicate the relative weight they attached to possible obstacles to holding domestic-currency-denominated bonds.

Question 6 asked respondents to indicate which obstacles made them *reluctant* to invest in bonds denominated in EL's currency. The potential obstacles as well as the corresponding mean and median answers are reported in Table A4: 1 is very important, 4 is not important.

Thus the factors that seem to make respondents more reluctant to invest in domestic-currency bonds include concerns about exchange rate manipulation and an unexpected rise in inflation. In additional comments, some respondents also cited concerns regarding the convertibility of the domestic currency (with the Russian GKOs case being recalled) and the domestic legal jurisdiction of local currency bonds. Interestingly, crossover investors seemed more willing to invest in local-currency instruments: their responses revealed uniformly less concern with all the possible factors that were suggested as deterrents to undertaking such investment.

References

Abiad, Abdul, and Ashoka Mody, 2003, "Financial Reform: What Shakes It? What Shapes It?" IMF Working Paper 03/70 (Washington: International Monetary Fund).

Aghion, Philippe, Philippe Bacchetta, and Abhijit Banerjee, 2001, "Currency Crises and Monetary Policy in a Credit-Constrained Economy," *European Economic Review*, Vol. 45, No. 7, pp. 1121–50.

Alesina, Alberto, Alessandro Prati, and Guido Tabellini, 1990, "Public Confidence and Debt Management: A Model and a Case Study of Italy," in *Public Debt Management: Theory and History*, ed. by Rudiger Dornbusch and Mario Draghi (Cambridge: Cambridge University Press), pp. 94–118.

Allen, Franklin, and Douglas Gale, 1994, *Financial Innovation and Risk Sharing* (Cambridge, Massachusetts: MIT Press).

Allen, Mark, 1988, "A Complementary Approach to the Debt Problem" (unpublished; Washington: International Monetary Fund).

———, Christoph B. Rosenberg, Christian Keller, Brad Setser, and Nouriel Roubini, 2002, "A Balance Sheet Approach to Financial Crisis," IMF Working Paper 02/210 (Washington: International Monetary Fund).

Arora, Vivek, and Athanasios Vamvakidis, 2004, "Trading Partners: How Much Do They Matter for Growth?" (unpublished; Washington: International Monetary Fund).

Asquith, Paul, and T.A. Wizman, 1990, "Event Risk, Covenants and Bondholder Returns in Leveraged Buyouts," *Journal of Financial Economics,* Vol. 27, pp. 195–213.

Athanasoulis, Stefano G., Robert J. Shiller, and Eric van Wincoop, 1999, "Macro Markets and Financial Security," *Federal Reserve Bank of New York Economic Policy Review*, Vol. 5, No. 1, pp. 21–39.

Bailey, Norman, 1983, "A Safety Net for Foreign Lending," *Business Week*, January 10.

Barclay, Michael, and Clifford Smith, 1995, "The Priority Structure of Corporate Liabilities," *Journal of Finance*, Vol. 50, No. 3, pp. 899–917.

Baron, Kevin, and Jeffrey Lange, 2003, "From Horses to Hedging," *Risk Magazine*, February. Available via the Internet: http://www.risk.net.

Barone, Emilio, and Rainer Masera, 1997, "Index-Linked Bonds from an Academic, Market and Policy-Making Standpoint," in *Managing Public Debt*, ed. by Marcello De Cecco, Lorenzo Pecchi, and Gustavo Piga (Cheltenham, United Kingdom: Edward Elgar), pp. 117–47.

Barro, Robert, 1995, "Optimal Debt Management," NBER Working Paper No. 5327 (Cambridge, Massachusetts: National Bureau of Economic Research).

Blejer, Mario I., and Adrienne Cheasty, 1991, "The Measurement of Fiscal Deficits: Analytical and Methodological Issues," *Journal of Economic Literature*, Vol. 29, No. 4, pp. 1644–78.

Bolton, Patrick, and David Skeel, 2003, "Inside the Black Box: How Should a Sovereign Bankruptcy Framework Be Structured?" (unpublished; Princeton, New Jersey: Princeton University).

Bolton, Patrick, and Olivier Jeanne, 2004, "Structuring and Restructuring Sovereign Debt: The Role of Seniority" (unpublished; Washington: International Monetary Fund).

Bordo, Michael, Barry Eichengreen, and Jongwoo Kim, 1998, "Was There Really an Earlier Period of International Financial Integration Comparable to Today?" NBER Working Paper No. 6738 (Cambridge, Massachusetts: National Bureau of Economic Research).

Bordo, Michael, Christopher Meissner, and Angela Redish, 2003, "How 'Original Sin' Was Overcome: The Evolution of External Debt Denominated in Domestic Currencies in the United States and the British Dominions," NBER Working Paper No. 9841 (Cambridge, Massachusetts: National Bureau of Economic Research).

Borensztein, Eduardo R., and Paolo Mauro, 2004, "The Case for GDP-Indexed Bonds," *Economic Policy* (April), pp. 165–216.

Boughton, James, 2001, *Silent Revolution: The International Monetary Fund, 1979–1989* (Washington: International Monetary Fund).

Buchheit, Lee C., and G. Mitu Gulati, 2002, "Sovereign Bonds and the Collective Will," *Emory Law Journal*, Vol. 51, No. 4, pp. 1317–64.

Burger, John D., and Frank E. Warnock, 2003, "Diversification, Original Sin, and International Bond Portfolios," International Finance Discussion Paper No. 755 (Washington: Board of Governors of the Federal Reserve System).

Bussière, Matthieu, and Christian Mulder, 1999, "External Vulnerability in Emerging Market Economies: How High Liquidity Can Offset Weak Fundamentals and the Effects of Contagion," IMF Working Paper 99/88 (Washington: International Monetary Fund).

Caballero, Ricardo, 2003, "Coping with Chile's External Vulnerability: A Financial Problem," in *Central Banking, Analysis, and Economic Policies*, Vol. 6 (Santiago: Banco Central de Chile).

———, Kevin Cowan, and Jonathan Kearns, 2003, "Dollar-Risk, Banks and Fear-of-Sudden-Stop: Lessons from Australia and Chile," paper presented at the Inter-American Development Bank conference, "Financial Dedollarization: Policy Options," December.

Calomiris, Charles W., and Charles M. Kahn, 1991, "The Role of Demandable Debt in Structuring Optimal Banking Arrangements," *American Economic Review*, Vol. 81, No. 3, pp. 497–513.

Calvo, Guillermo, 1988, "Servicing the Public Debt: The Role of Expectations," *American Economic Review,* Vol. 78, No. 4, pp. 647–61.

———, 2003, "Explaining Sudden Stop, Growth Collapse, and BOP Crisis: The Case of Distortionary Output Taxes," *Staff Papers,* International Monetary Fund, Vol. 50 (Special Issue), pp. 1–20.

———, and Pablo Guidotti, 1990, "Indexation and Maturity of the Government Bonds: An Exploratory Model," in *Public Debt Management: Theory and History*, ed. by Rudiger Dornbusch and Mario Draghi (Cambridge: Cambridge University Press), pp. 52–93.

Campbell, J.Y., and R.J. Shiller, 1996, "A Scorecard for Indexed Government Debt," in *NBER Macroeconomics Annual 1996*, ed. by Ben S. Bernanke and Julio R. Rotemberg, pp. 155–97.

Carson, Carol S., S. Khawaja, and T. Morrison, 2004, "Revisions Policy for Official Statistics: A Matter of Governance," IMF Working Paper 04/87 (Washington: International Monetary Fund).

Caselli, Francesco, and Priyanka Malhotra, 2004, "National Disasters and Growth: From Thought Experiment to National Experiment" (unpublished: Washington: International Monetary Fund).

Cashin, Paul A., Hong Liang, and C. John McDermott, 2000, "How Persistent Are Shocks to World Commodity Prices? *Staff Papers*, International Monetary Fund, Vol. 47, pp. 177–217.

Chalk, Nigel A., 2002, "The Potential Role for Securitizing Public Sector Revenue Flows: An Application to the Philippines," IMF Working Paper 02/106 (Washington: International Monetary Fund).

Chamon, Marcos, 2002, "Why Can't Developing Countries Borrow from Abroad in Their Currency?" Social Science Research Network Electronic Library Working Paper.

———, 2004, "Can Debt Crises Be Self-Fulfilling?" IMF Working Paper 04/99 (Washington: International Monetary Fund).

Claessens, Stijn, and Ronald C. Duncan, 1993, *Managing Commodity Price Risk in Developing Countries* (Baltimore, Maryland: Johns Hopkins University Press).

Claessens, Stijn, Daniela Klingebiel, and Sergio Schmukler, 2003, "Government Bonds in Domestic and Foreign-Currency: The Role of Macroeconomic and Institutional Factors" (unpublished; Washington: World Bank).

Cole, Harold, and Patrick Kehoe, 2000, "Self-Fulfilling Debt Crises," *The Review of Economic Studies*, Vol. 67, pp. 91–116.

Collier, Paul, and Jan Dehn, 2001, "Aid, Shocks, and Growth," Policy Research Working Paper 2688 (Washington: World Bank).

Daniel, James, 2001, "Hedging Government Oil Price Risk," IMF Working Paper 01/185 (Washington: International Monetary Fund).

Davis, Jeffrey, Rolando Ossowski, James Daniel, and Steven Barnett, 2001, *Stabilization and Savings Funds for Nonrenewable Resources*, IMF Occasional Paper No. 205 (Washington: International Monetary Fund).

Deacon, Mark, and Andre Derry, 1998, *Inflation-Indexed Securities* (London: Prentice Hall).

Dehn, Jan, Christopher L. Gilbert, and Panos Varangis, "Agricultural Commodity Price Volatility," in *Managing Economic Volatility and Crises: A Practitioner's Guide* (forthcoming; Cambridge: Cambridge University Press).

Detragiache, Enrica, 1994, "Sensible Buybacks of Sovereign Debt," *Journal of Development Economics*, Vol. 43, pp. 317–33.

———, and Antonio Spilimbergo, 2001, "Crises and Liquidity: Evidence and Interpretation," IMF Working Paper 01/2 (Washington: International Monetary Fund).

Diamond, Douglas W., 1991, "Debt Maturity Structure and Liquidity Risk," *Quarterly Journal of Economics*, Vol. 106, No. 3, pp. 709–37.

———, 1993, "Seniority and Maturity of Debt Contracts," *Journal of Financial Economics*, Vol. 33, No. 3, pp. 341–68.

———, and Raghuram Rajan, 2001, "Banks, Short-Term Debt, and Financial Crises: Theory, Policy Implications and Applications," *Journal of Monetary Economics*, Proceedings of the Carnegie-Rochester Conference on Public Policy, Vol. 54, pp. 37–71.

Dooley, Michael P., 2000, "Can Output Losses Following International Financial Crises Be Avoided?" NBER Working Paper No. 7531 (Cambridge, Massachusetts: National Bureau of Economic Research).

———, and Sujata Verma, 2001, "Rescue Packages and Output Losses Following Crises," NBER Working Paper No. 8315 (Cambridge, Massachusetts: National Bureau of Economic Research).

Drèze, Jacques H., 2000a, "Globalisation and Securitisation of Risk Bearing," CORE (unpublished; Université Catholique de Louvain, Belgium). Available via the Internet: www.core.ucl.ac.be/staff/dreze.html.

———, 2000b, "Economic and Social Security in the Twenty-First Century, with Attention to Europe," *Scandinavian Journal of Economics*, Vol. 102, No. 3, pp. 327–48.

Easterly, William R., 2001, "Growth Implosions and Debt Explosions: Do Growth Slowdowns Cause Public Debt Crises?" *Contributions to Macroeconomics*, Vol. 1, No. 1, Article 1 (Berkeley, California: Electronic Press). Available via the Internet: http://www.bepress.com/bejm/contributions/vol1/iss1/art1.

———, Michael Kremer, Lant Pritchett, and Lawrence H. Summers, 1993, "Good Policy or Good Luck? Country Growth Performance and Temporary Shocks," *Journal of Monetary Economics*, Vol. 32, pp. 459–83.

Eaton, Jonathan, 2002, "Standstills and an International Bankruptcy Court," paper presented at the Bank of

England conference, "The Role of the Official and Private Sectors in Resolving International Financial Crises," July.

———, and Raquel Fernandez, 1997, "Sovereign Debt," in *Handbook of International Economics*, ed. by Gene Grossman and Kenneth Rogoff (Amsterdam; New York and Oxford: Elsevier, North-Holland), pp. 2031–77.

Eichengreen, Barry, Ricardo Hausmann, and Ugo Panizza, 2002, "Original Sin: The Pain, the Mystery, and the Road to Redemption," in *Debt Denomination and Financial Instability in Emerging Market Economies*, ed. by Barry Eichengreen and Ricardo Hausmann (Chicago: University of Chicago Press).

Eichengreen, Barry, and Ashoka Mody, 1998, "What Explains Changing Spreads on Emerging-Market Debt: Fundamentals or Market Sentiment?" NBER Working Paper No. 6408 (Cambridge, Massachusetts: National Bureau of Economic Research).

Englund, Peter, Torbjorn Becker, and Anders Paalzow, 1997, *Public Debt Management (Statsskuldspolitiken,* in Swedish with English summary), Statens Offentliga Utredningar, Vol. 66 (Stockholm: Ministry of Finance).

Falcetti, Elisabetta, and Alessandro Missale, 2002, "Public Debt Indexation and Denomination with an Independent Central Bank," *European Economic Review*, Vol. 46, pp. 1825–50.

Fama, Eugene F., and Merton H. Miller, 1972, *The Theory of Finance* (New York: Holt, Rinehart and Winston).

Fischer, Bernhard, and Helmut Reisen, 1994, "Pension Fund Investment from Aging to Emerging Markets," Policy Brief No. 9 (Paris: OECD Development Centre).

Flandreau, Marc, and Nathan Sussman, 2002, "Old Sins: Exchange Clauses and European Foreign Lending in the 19th Century," in *Debt Denomination and Financial Instability in Emerging Market Economies*, ed. by Barry Eichengreen and Ricardo Hausmann (Chicago: University of Chicago Press).

Fontenay, Patrick de, Gian Maria Milesi-Ferretti, and Huw Pill, 1997, "The Role of Foreign-Currency Debt in Public Debt Management," in *Macroeconomic Dimensions of Public Finance, Essays in Honour of Vito Tanzi,* ed. by Mario I. Blejer and Teresa Ter-Minassian (London and New York: Routledge), pp. 203–32.

Franks, Julian, and Walter Torous, 1989, "An Empirical Investigation of U.S. Firms in Reorganization," *Journal of Finance,* Vol. 44, No. 3, pp. 747–69.

Freeman, Paul, Michael J. Keen, and Muthukumara Mani, 2003, "Dealing with Increased Risk of Natural Disasters: Challenges and Options," IMF Working Paper 03/197 (Washington: International Monetary Fund).

Freeman, Paul, Leslie A. Martin, Joanne Linneroot-Bayer, Reinhard Mechler, Georg Pflug, Koko Warner, 2003, *Disaster Risk Management* (Washington: Inter-American Development Bank).

Froot, Kenneth A., David S. Scharfstein, and Jeremy Stein, 1989, "LDC Debt: Forgiveness, Indexation, and Investment Incentives," *Journal of Finance*, Vol. 44, No. 5, pp. 1335–50.

Galindo, Arturo, and Leonardo Leiderman, 2003, "Living with Dollarization and the Route to Dedollarization," paper presented at the Inter-American Development Bank conference, "Financial Dedollarization: Policy Options," December.

Gavin, Michael, and Roberto Perotti, 1997, "Fiscal Policy in Latin America," in *NBER Macroeconomics Annual*, ed. by Ben Bernanke and Julio Rotenberg (Cambridge, Massachusetts: MIT Press), pp. 11–61.

Gelpern, Anna, 2004, "Building a Better Seating Chart of Sovereign Restructurings" (unpublished; Washington: Council on Foreign Relations), June.

Gilbert, Roy, and Alcira Kreimer, 1999, "Learning from the World Bank's Experience of Natural Disaster Related Assistance," Urban and Local Government Working Paper No. 2 (Washington: World Bank).

Goldstein, Morris, and Philip Turner, 2004, *Controlling Currency Mismatches in Emerging Markets* (Washington: Institute for International Economics).

Goyal, Vidhan K., 2003, "Market Discipline of Bank Risk: Evidence from Subordinated Debt Contracts" (unpublished; Hong Kong: University of Science and Technology).

Guidotti, Pablo, and Manmohan Kumar, 1991, *Domestic Public Debt of Externally Indebted Countries*, IMF Occasional Paper No. 80 (Washington: International Monetary Fund).

Haldane, Andy, 1999, "Private Sector Involvement in Financial Crisis: Analytics and Public Policy Approaches," *Financial Stability Review*, Issue No. 7, pp. 184–202. Available via the Internet: http://www.bankofengland.co.uk/fsr/fsr07.htm.

Hart, Oliver, 1995, *Firms, Contracts, and Financial Structure* (Oxford: Clarendon Press).

———, and John Moore, 1995, "Debt and Seniority: An Analysis of the Role of Hard Claims in Constraining Management," *American Economic Review*, Vol. 85 (June), pp. 567–85.

Hausmann, Ricardo, and Ugo Panizza, 2002, "The Mystery of Original Sin: The Case of the Missing Apple," in *Debt Denomination and Financial Instability in Emerging Market Economies*, ed. by Barry Eichengreen and Ricardo Hausmann (Chicago: University of Chicago Press).

Herrera, Luis, and Rodrigo Valdés, 2003, "Dedollarization, Indexation and Nominalization: The Chilean Experience," paper presented at the Inter-American Development Bank conference, "Financial Dedollarization: Policy Options," December.

Hoffmaister, Alexander W., and Jorge E. Roldós, 1997, "Are Business Cycles Different in Asia and Latin America?" IMF Working Paper 97/9 (Washington: International Monetary Fund).

Hull, John C., 2002, *Fundamentals of Futures and Options Markets* (Upper Saddle River, New Jersey: Prentice Hall).

International Monetary Fund, 1995, *International Capital Markets Report: Developments, Prospects, and Policy Issues* (Washington: International Monetary Fund), August.

———, 2000a, "Debt- and Reserve-Related Indicators of External Vulnerability." Available via the Internet: http://www.imf.org/external/np/pdr/debtres.

————, 2000b, "The Impact of Higher Oil Prices on the Global Economy." Available via the Internet: http://www.imf.org/external/pubs/cat/longres.cfm?sk& sk =3865.0.

————, 2002a, "Sovereign Debt Restructurings and the Domestic Economy: Experience in Four Recent Cases." Available via the Internet: http://www.imf. org/external/NP/pdr/sdrm/2002/022102.pdf.

————, 2002b, "The Design of the Sovereign Debt Restructuring Mechanism—Further Considerations." Available via the Internet: http://www.imf.org/ external/np/pdr/sdrm/2002/112702.htm.

————, 2003a, "Sustainability Assessments—Review of Application and Methodological Refinements." Available via the internet: www:imf.org/external/np/pdr/ sustain/2003/061003.htm.

————, 2003b, "Crisis Resolution in the Context of Sovereign Debt Restructuring—A Summary of Considerations." Available via the Internet: www.imf.org/ external/np/pdr/sdrm/2003/012803.htm.

————, 2003c, *External Debt Statistics, Guide for Compilers and Users* (Washington: International Monetary Fund). Also available via the Internet: http://www.imf.org/external/pubs/ft/eds/Eng/Guide/ index.htm.

————, 2003d, "Assessing Public Sector Borrowing Collateralized on Future Flow Receivables," June. Available via the Internet: http://www.imf.org/external/np/ fad/2003/061103.htm.

————, 2003e, *Global Financial Stability Report*, World Economic and Financial Surveys (Washington: International Monetary Fund).

————, 2003f, "Lessons from the Crisis in Argentina." Available via the Internet: http//www.imf.org/external/np/pdr/lessons/100803.htm.

————, 2003g, "Collective Action Clauses: Recent Developments and Issues." Available via the Internet: http://www.imf.org/external/np/psi/2003/032503.pdf.

————, and World Bank, 2001, *Guidelines on Public Debt Management* (Washington: International Monetary Fund and World Bank).

————, 2003, *Guidelines for Public Debt Management: Accompanying Document and Selected Case Studies* (Washington: International Monetary Fund and World Bank).

Ize, Alain, and Eric Parrado, 2002, "Dollarization, Monetary Policy, and the Pass-Through," IMF Working Paper 02/188 (Washington: International Monetary Fund).

Jeanne, Olivier, 2000, "Foreign-Currency Debt and the Global Financial Architecture," *European Economic Review*, Papers and Proceedings, Vol. 44, pp. 719–27.

————, 2003, "Why Do Emerging Market Economies Borrow in Foreign Currency?" IMF Working Paper 03/177 (Washington: International Monetary Fund).

————, 2004, "Debt Maturity and the International Financial Architecture," IMF Working Paper 04/137 (Washington: International Monetary Fund).

————, and Jeromin Zettelmeyer, 2002, "Original Sin: Balance Sheet Crises and the Roles of International Lending," IMF Working Paper 02/234 (Washington: International Monetary Fund).

Kaeser, Daniel, 1990, "Pour un système équitable de désendettement," speech given at a Swissaid Forum on Solutions to the Debt Crisis, October, available from the author; shorter versions of the speech were published in *Schweizerische Handelszeitung*, April 5, 1990, and *Domaine Public*, November 1, 1990.

Kaufmann, Daniel, Aart Kraay, and M. Mastruzzi, 2003, "Governance Matters III: Governance Indicators for 1996–2002," World Bank Policy Research Working Paper 2196 (Washington: World Bank).

Kletzer, Kenneth M, 1984, "Asymmetries of Information and LDC Borrowing with Sovereign Risk," *Economic Journal*, Vol. 94, No. 374, pp. 287–307.

Kopcke, Richard W., and Ralph C. Kimball, 1999, "Inflation-Indexed Bonds: The Dog That Didn't Bark," Federal Reserve Bank of Boston, *New England Economic Review*, pp. 3–24.

Kraay, Aart, and Vikram Nehru, 2003, "When Is Debt Sustainable?" (unpublished; Washington: World Bank).

Kroszner, Randall, 1999, "Is It Better to Forgive Than to Receive? Evidence from the Abrogation of Gold Index Clauses in Long-Term Debt During the Great Depression" (unpublished; Chicago: University of Chicago). Available via the Internet: http://gsbwww. uchicago.edu/fac/randall.kroszner/research.

Krugman, Paul, 1988, "Financing vs. Forgiving a Debt Overhang," *Journal of Development Economics*, Vol. 29, pp. 253–68.

————, 1999, "Balance Sheets, The Transfer Problem, and Financial Crises" in *International Finance and Financial Crises, Essays in Honor of Robert P. Flood*, ed. by Peter Isard and Andrew Rose (Dordrecht, Netherlands: Kluwer).

Lasfer, M. Ameziane, 1999, "Debt Structure, Agency Costs and Firm's Size: An Empirical Investigation" (unpublished; London: City University Business School).

Lessard, Donald R., and John Williamson, 1985, "Financial Intermediation Beyond the Debt Crisis" (unpublished; Washington: Institute for International Economics).

Levy-Yeyati, Eduardo, 2003, "Una propuesta para desdolarizar," *La Nación*, October 19.

Lipworth, Gabrielle, and Jens Nystedt, 2001, "Crisis Resolution and Private Sector Adaptation," *Staff Papers*, International Monetary Fund, Vol. 47 (Special Issue), pp. 188–214.

Manasse, Paolo, Nouriel Roubini, and Axel Schimmelpfennig, 2003, "Predicting Sovereign Debt Crises," IMF Working Paper 03/221 (Washington: International Monetary Fund).

Mauro, Paolo, Nathan Sussman, and Yishay Yafeh, 2002, "Emerging Market Spreads: Then Versus Now," *Quarterly Journal of Economics*, Vol. 117, No. 2, pp. 695–733.

Mauro, Paolo, and Yishay Yafeh, 2003, "The Corporation of Foreign Bondholders," IMF Working Paper 03/107 (Washington: International Monetary Fund).

Missale, Alessandro, 1999, *Public Debt Management* (Oxford: Oxford University Press).

North, Douglass, and Barry Weingast, 1989, "Constitutions and Commitment: The Evolution of Institutions Governing Public Choice in Seventeenth-Century

England," *Journal of Economic History*, Vol. 49, No. 4, pp. 803–32.

Obstfeld, Maurice, and Giovanni Peri, 1998, "Regional Nonadjustment and Fiscal Policy," in *EMU: Prospects and Challenges for the Euro* (Special Issue of *Economic Policy*), ed. by David Begg, Jürgen von Hagen, Charles Wyplosz, and Klaus F. Zimmermann.

Price, Robert, 1997, "The Rationale and Design of Inflation-Indexed Bonds," IMF Working Paper 97/12 (Washington: International Monetary Fund).

Reinhart, Carmen, Kenneth Rogoff, and Miguel Savastano, 2003, "Debt Intolerance," *Brookings Papers on Economic Activity: 1*, Brookings Institution, pp. 1–74.

Rodrik, Daniel, and Andrés Velasco, 1999, "Short-Term Capital Flows," NBER Working Paper No. 7364 (Cambridge, Massachusetts: National Bureau of Economic Research).

Rogoff, Kenneth, 1999, "International Institutions for Reducing Global Financial Instability," *Journal of Economic Perspectives*, Vol. 13, pp. 21–42.

Sachs, Jeffrey, 1984, "Theoretical Issues in International Borrowing," *Princeton Studies in International Finance,* Vol. 54 (Princeton, New Jersey: Princeton University).

———, and Daniel Cohen, 1982, "LDC Borrowing with Default Risk," NBER Working Paper No. 925 (Cambridge, Massachusetts: National Bureau of Economic Research).

Shiller, Robert J., 1993, *Macro Markets: Creating Institutions for Managing Society's Largest Economic Risks* (Oxford: Clarendon Press).

———, 2003, *The New Financial Order: Risk in the 21st Century* (Oxford and Princeton, New Jersey: Princeton University Press).

Smith, C.W., Jr., and J. Warner, 1979, "On Financial Contracting: An Analysis of Bond Covenants," *Journal of Financial Economics*, Vol. 7, No. 2, pp. 117–61.

Talvi, Ernesto, and Carlos Végh, 2002, "Tax Base Variability and Procyclical Fiscal Policy," NBER Working Paper No. 7499 (Cambridge, Massachusetts: National Bureau of Economic Research).

Tirole, Jean, 2002, *Financial Crises, Liquidity, and the International Monetary System* (Princeton, New Jersey: Princeton University Press).

United Nations Conference on Trade and Development (UNCTAD), 2001, COMTRADE, Geneva.

Varsavsky, Martín, and Miguel Braun, 2002, "¿Cuánto interés tienen que pagar los bonos argentinos?" *La Nación*, February 4. Available via the Internet: http://www.lanacion.com.ar/02/02/04/de_371608.asp.

Weiss, Lawrence A., 1990, "Bankruptcy Resolution: Direct Costs and Violation of Priority of Claims, *Journal of Financial Economics,* Vol. 27, No. 2, pp. 285–314.

Werner, Alejandro, 2003, "Undoing and Avoiding Dollarization," paper presented at the Inter-American Development Bank conference, "Financial Dedollarization: Policy Options," December.

Wilde, Oscar, 1906, *The Canterville Ghost: An Amusing Chronicle of the Tribulations of the Ghost of Canterville Chase When His Ancestral Halls Became the Home of the American Minister to the Court of St. James* (Boston: J.W. Luce).

Zettelmeyer, Jeromin, "The Case for an Explicit Seniority Structure in Sovereign Debt," IMF Working Paper (forthcoming; Washington: International Monetary Fund).

Recent Occasional Papers of the International Monetary Fund

237. Sovereign Debt Structure for Crisis Prevention, by Eduardo Borensztein, Marcos Chamon, Olivier Jeanne, Paolo Mauro, and Jeromin Zettelmeyer. 2004.

236. Lessons from the Crisis in Argentina, by Christina Daseking, Atish R. Ghosh, Alun Thomas, and Timothy Lane. 2004.

235. A New Look at Exchange Rate Volatility and Trade Flows, by Peter B. Clark, Natalia Tamirisa, and Shang-Jin Wei, with Azim Sadikov and Li Zeng. 2004.

234. Adopting the Euro in Central Europe: Challenges of the Next Step in European Integration, by Susan M. Schadler, Paulo F. Drummond, Louis Kuijs, Zuzana Murgasova, and Rachel N. van Elkan. 2004.

233. Germany's Three-Pillar Banking System: Cross-Country Perspectives in Europe, by Allan Brunner, Jörg Decressin, Daniel Hardy, and Beata Kudela. 2004.

232. China's Growth and Integration into the World Economy: Prospects and Challenges, edited by Eswar Prasad. 2004.

231. Chile: Policies and Institutions Underpinning Stability and Growth, by Eliot Kalter, Steven Phillips, Marco A. Espinosa-Vega, Rodolfo Luzio, Mauricio Villafuerte, and Manmohan Singh. 2004.

230. Financial Stability in Dollarized Countries, by Anne-Marie Gulde, David Hoelscher, Alain Ize, David Marston, and Gianni De Nicoló. 2004.

229. Evolution and Performance of Exchange Rate Regimes, by Kenneth S. Rogoff, Aasim M. Husain, Ashoka Mody, Robin Brooks, and Nienke Oomes. 2004.

228. Capital Markets and Financial Intermediation in The Baltics, by Alfred Schipke, Christian Beddies, Susan M. George, and Niamh Sheridan. 2004.

227. U.S. Fiscal Policies and Priorities for Long-Run Sustainability, edited by Martin Mühleisen and Christopher Towe. 2004.

226. Hong Kong SAR: Meeting the Challenges of Integration with the Mainland, edited by Eswar Prasad, with contributions from Jorge Chan-Lau, Dora Iakova, William Lee, Hong Liang, Ida Liu, Papa N'Diaye, and Tao Wang. 2004.

225. Rules-Based Fiscal Policy in France, Germany, Italy, and Spain, by Teresa Dában, Enrica Detragiache, Gabriel di Bella, Gian Maria Milesi-Ferretti, and Steven Symansky. 2003.

224. Managing Systemic Banking Crises, by a staff team led by David S. Hoelscher and Marc Quintyn. 2003.

223. Monetary Union Among Member Countries of the Gulf Cooperation Council, by a staff team led by Ugo Fasano. 2003.

222. Informal Funds Transfer Systems: An Analysis of the Informal Hawala System, by Mohammed El Qorchi, Samuel Munzele Maimbo, and John F. Wilson. 2003.

221. Deflation: Determinants, Risks, and Policy Options, by Manmohan S. Kumar. 2003.

220. Effects of Financial Globalization on Developing Countries: Some Empirical Evidence, by Eswar S. Prasad, Kenneth Rogoff, Shang-Jin Wei, and Ayhan Kose. 2003.

219. Economic Policy in a Highly Dollarized Economy: The Case of Cambodia, by Mario de Zamaroczy and Sopanha Sa. 2003.

218. Fiscal Vulnerability and Financial Crises in Emerging Market Economies, by Richard Hemming, Michael Kell, and Axel Schimmelpfennig. 2003.

217. Managing Financial Crises: Recent Experience and Lessons for Latin America, edited by Charles Collyns and G. Russell Kincaid. 2003.

216. Is the PRGF Living Up to Expectations?—An Assessment of Program Design, by Sanjeev Gupta, Mark Plant, Benedict Clements, Thomas Dorsey, Emanuele Baldacci, Gabriela Inchauste, Shamsuddin Tareq, and Nita Thacker. 2002.

215. Improving Large Taxpayers' Compliance: A Review of Country Experience, by Katherine Baer. 2002.

214. Advanced Country Experiences with Capital Account Liberalization, by Age Bakker and Bryan Chapple. 2002.

213. The Baltic Countries: Medium-Term Fiscal Issues Related to EU and NATO Accession, by Johannes Mueller, Christian Beddies, Robert Burgess, Vitali Kramarenko, and Joannes Mongardini. 2002.

212. Financial Soundness Indicators: Analytical Aspects and Country Practices, by V. Sundararajan, Charles Enoch, Armida San José, Paul Hilbers, Russell Krueger, Marina Moretti, and Graham Slack. 2002.

211. Capital Account Liberalization and Financial Sector Stability, by a staff team led by Shogo Ishii and Karl Habermeier. 2002.

210. IMF-Supported Programs in Capital Account Crises, by Atish Ghosh, Timothy Lane, Marianne Schulze-Ghattas, Aleš Bulíř, Javier Hamann, and Alex Mourmouras. 2002.

209. Methodology for Current Account and Exchange Rate Assessments, by Peter Isard, Hamid Faruqee, G. Russell Kincaid, and Martin Fetherston. 2001.

208. Yemen in the 1990s: From Unification to Economic Reform, by Klaus Enders, Sherwyn Williams, Nada Choueiri, Yuri Sobolev, and Jan Walliser. 2001.

207. Malaysia: From Crisis to Recovery, by Kanitta Meesook, Il Houng Lee, Olin Liu, Yougesh Khatri, Natalia Tamirisa, Michael Moore, and Mark H. Krysl. 2001.

206. The Dominican Republic: Stabilization, Structural Reform, and Economic Growth, by a staff team led by Philip Young comprising Alessandro Giustiniani, Werner C. Keller, and Randa E. Sab and others. 2001.

205. Stabilization and Savings Funds for Nonrenewable Resources, by Jeffrey Davis, Rolando Ossowski, James Daniel, and Steven Barnett. 2001.

204. Monetary Union in West Africa (ECOWAS): Is It Desirable and How Could It Be Achieved? by Paul Masson and Catherine Pattillo. 2001.

203. Modern Banking and OTC Derivatives Markets: The Transformation of Global Finance and Its Implications for Systemic Risk, by Garry J. Schinasi, R. Sean Craig, Burkhard Drees, and Charles Kramer. 2000.

202. Adopting Inflation Targeting: Practical Issues for Emerging Market Countries, by Andrea Schaechter, Mark R. Stone, and Mark Zelmer. 2000.

201. Developments and Challenges in the Caribbean Region, by Samuel Itam, Simon Cueva, Erik Lundback, Janet Stotsky, and Stephen Tokarick. 2000.

200. Pension Reform in the Baltics: Issues and Prospects, by Jerald Schiff, Niko Hobdari, Axel Schimmel-pfennig, and Roman Zytek. 2000.

199. Ghana: Economic Development in a Democratic Environment, by Sérgio Pereira Leite, Anthony Pellechio, Luisa Zanforlin, Girma Begashaw, Stefania Fabrizio, and Joachim Harnack. 2000.

198. Setting Up Treasuries in the Baltics, Russia, and Other Countries of the Former Soviet Union: An Assessment of IMF Technical Assistance, by Barry H. Potter and Jack Diamond. 2000.

197. Deposit Insurance: Actual and Good Practices, by Gillian G.H. Garcia. 2000.

196. Trade and Trade Policies in Eastern and Southern Africa, by a staff team led by Arvind Subramanian, with Enrique Gelbard, Richard Harmsen, Katrin Elborgh-Woytek, and Piroska Nagy. 2000.

195. The Eastern Caribbean Currency Union—Institutions, Performance, and Policy Issues, by Frits van Beek, José Roberto Rosales, Mayra Zermeño, Ruby Randall, and Jorge Shepherd. 2000.

194. Fiscal and Macroeconomic Impact of Privatization, by Jeffrey Davis, Rolando Ossowski, Thomas Richardson, and Steven Barnett. 2000.

193. Exchange Rate Regimes in an Increasingly Integrated World Economy, by Michael Mussa, Paul Masson, Alexander Swoboda, Esteban Jadresic, Paolo Mauro, and Andy Berg. 2000.

192. Macroprudential Indicators of Financial System Soundness, by a staff team led by Owen Evans, Alfredo M. Leone, Mahinder Gill, and Paul Hilbers. 2000.

191. Social Issues in IMF-Supported Programs, by Sanjeev Gupta, Louis Dicks-Mireaux, Ritha Khemani, Calvin McDonald, and Marijn Verhoeven. 2000.

190. Capital Controls: Country Experiences with Their Use and Liberalization, by Akira Ariyoshi, Karl Habermeier, Bernard Laurens, Inci Ötker-Robe, Jorge Iván Canales Kriljenko, and Andrei Kirilenko. 2000.

Note: For information on the titles and availability of Occasional Papers not listed, please consult the IMF's *Publications Catalog* or contact IMF Publication Services.